# "I Have Got Something To Say, But I Don't Know Your Language Yet!"

# Lesley College Series in Arts and Education

Elijah Mirochnik
*General Editor*

Vol. 2

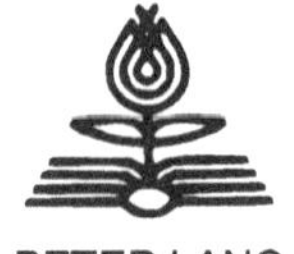

PETER LANG
New York • Washington, D.C./Baltimore • Boston • Bern
Frankfurt am Main • Berlin • Brussels • Vienna • Oxford

Elisabeth K. Hösli

# "I Have Got Something To Say, But I Don't Know Your Language Yet!"

## Intermodal Learning in Multicultural Urban Education

PETER LANG
New York • Washington, D.C./Baltimore • Boston • Bern
Frankfurt am Main • Berlin • Brussels • Vienna • Oxford

**Library of Congress Cataloging-in-Publication Data**

Hösli, Elisabeth K.
"I have got something to say, but I don't know your language yet!":
intermodal learning in multicultural urban education / Elisabeth K. Hösli.
p. cm. — (Lesley College series in arts and education; vol. 2)
Includes bibliographical references.
1. Children of immigrants—Education—Switzerland—Zurich.
2. Education, Urban—Switzerland—Zurich. 3. Multicultural
education—Switzerland—Zurich. I. Title. II. Series.
LC3747.S9H67 371.826'91—dc21 99-34387
ISBN 0-8204-4587-8
ISSN 1524-0177

**Die Deutsche Bibliothek-CIP-Einheitsaufnahme**

Hösli, Elisabeth K.:
"I have got something to say, but I don't know your language yet!": intermodal learning in
multicultural urban education / Elisabeth K. Hösli.
–New York; Washington, D.C./Baltimore; Boston; Bern;
Frankfurt am Main; Berlin; Brussels; Vienna; Oxford: Lang.
(Lesley College series in arts and education; Vol. 2)
ISBN 0-8204-4587-8

Cover design by Nona Reuter



Printed in the United States of America

I dedicate my book to all children, for every child has something to say.
Everyone—there is no exception.

# Table of Contents


**List of Tables** ix
**List of Figures** xi
**List of Photographs** xiii
**Acknowledgments** xv
**Preface** xvii

**1. Children with Foreign Mother Tongues** 1
Context 1
Multiculturalism and Education 5
Working with Immigrant Children 11

**2. Intermodal Learning** 15
Aspects and Phases of Intermodal Learning 17
Important Principles of Intermodal Learning in Education 20
Construction of Realities in *Four Languages* 23
Requirements for Significant Subjects 25
Goals of Intermodal Learning 26

**3. Didactics within Multicultural Contexts** 29
First Example: Mask Project 30
Second Example: Opposites 41
Third Example: Intermodal Learning 49
Development of Language—A Summary 53

**4. Theoretical Frames** 57
An Art Orientated Approach 57
Levels of Language Proficiency 60
The Theory of Multiple Intelligences 64

The Intermodal Method and the Method of Working with Core Ideas 68
The Underlying Concept of Development 71
The Concept of Education 77

**5. Concluding Reflections** **83**

**Appendix** **87**
1. The Mask Project 87
2. The Subject of Opposites 90
3. Intermodal Processes 92

**Notes** **97**

**Bibliography** **99**

# Tables


Table 1: Frames in Intermodal Learning 22

Table 2: The *Four Languages* 24

Table 3: The Multiple Intelligences I 65

Table 4: The Multiple Intelligences II 67

Table 5: Concept of Education 79

# Figures

Figure 1: Aspects and Phases of Intermodal Learning 18

Figure 2: Hierarchy of Needs According to Maslow 53

Figure 3: Surface and Deeper Levels of Language Proficiency 61

Figure 4: The '*dual iceberg*' Representation of Bilingual Proficiency 63

# Photographs


Photograph 1: "The Bird Is Flying to Sri Lanka" 10

Photograph 2: Dobrinka on Her First Day 14

Photograph 3: Miri, the Crying Mask 33

Photograph 4: Queen Mitri 34

Photograph 5: Tschim's Performance with the Chair 35

Photograph 6: Opposites I 44

Photograph 7: Opposites II 45

Photograph 8: Ismail's Sketch of His Mask 51

Photograph 9: Nuran as Cimona on Stage 85

# Acknowledgments

I would like to give warm thanks to all who in some way accompanied and supported me through the process of writing this book. First, I would like to mention Brigitte and Peter Wanzenried, who introduced me to the International School for Interdisciplinary Studies (ISIS) in Zurich, and to Lesley College. Our long-standing friendship has taken on a new perspective and intensity. Vera Decurtins, who in addition to Debbie Sherman and Peter Wanzenried was one of my team members for my Independent Study Degree Program at Lesley College, gave me the initial impetus to start my studies. Without her this book wouldn't have been written. As a teacher and expert on expressive therapy and education, and as a remedial educator working with preschool immigrant children, she gave me invaluable direction and encouragement. Peter Wanzenried is a professor at the basic teachers' training college of the Canton of Zurich and the leader of the educational section of ISIS courses in Zurich. In this latter capacity he introduced me to the theory and method of intermodal learning. His tremendously creative skills in constructing and teaching theories and methods has had a great influence on me and my work. I especially thank him for his poetical contributions to this book, and the permission to reprint a figure and a table from his unpublished papers. Debbie Sherman helped to hold our team together and with our connection to Lesley College. I loved her open-mindedness toward my theme and toward our specific Swiss style of thinking and researching. Since the beginning of my studies, she has motivated me to write this book. It is thanks to her efforts and commitment this book is now a reality. Further, I would like to thank my partners at school, Gabi Trinkler and Anita Kubli, whose flexibility enabled me to attend the ISIS course. I am grateful to all teachers who attended the in-service courses and, therefore, helped me to reflect and extend my knowledge and experience through their shared experiences and personal contributions. I'd like also to thank all my friends and members of my family who supported me emotionally and intellectually during my studies and the period of writing this book. Last, but not least, I give a warm thank you to all my students for their invaluable contributions. I hope that they can find their place in our community and will become strong members of our society.

Grateful acknowledgement is hereby made to copyright holders for permission to use the following copyrighted material:

Cummins Jim, *Bilingualism and Special Education: Issues in Assessment and Pedagogy*. Clevedon, Avon, England: Multilingual Matters, © 1984. Reprinted by permission of the publisher. All rights reserved.

Nodari Claudio, *Deutsch für fremdsprachige Kinder; Theoretischer Teil; Grundlagen für den Unterricht*. Aarau, Switzerland: Interkantonale Lehrmittelzentrale, Lehrmittelverlag des Kantons Aargau, © 1989. Reprinted by permission of the publisher. All rights reserved.

# Preface

"If you take away a people's language, it's effectively genocide."[1] This statement roused me to action. Immediately, I understood that these words would change my way of teaching in a fundamental way. This was in 1992, and for the previous nine years I had been teaching a special integration class for non-German speaking immigrant children, called *Kleinklasse E*, in the city of Zurich.

Zurich is the largest city in Switzerland and its economic heart. Still, the city and its suburbs with a million inhabitants is a rather small city. Zurich is located in the German part of Switzerland; therefore the spoken language is a Swiss-German dialect. At school, we all have to learn High German as a first foreign language. The written language is High German as well. I used to work in the most underprivileged district of this quite rich town; underprivileged, because the area is known as the red-light district of Zurich, because of the alcohol and drug scene (which fortunately has declined in the last three years), because of a bad traffic situation, and because of the lack of playgrounds. The area is inhabited by a majority of socially, economically, and educationally deprived people, most badly integrated into Swiss mainstream society, Swiss as well as foreigners. The majority of the inhabitants are immigrants, people from the whole world; a multi-cultural melting pot with all its advantages and disadvantages.

Due to the many language differences, I found my students cut off from verbal expression for the first months of school, but I felt nevertheless that they shouldn't grow numb and lose hope in their new surrounding. In 1992, I was introduced to the intermodal expressive method in therapy, counseling, and education. The core of the method of intermodal learning is the natural use of different art disciplines of visual art, music, dance, literature, and theater. It motivates expression not only verbally but in a variety of other kinds of *languages*. I was fascinated by the variety, the sense, and the meaningfulness of the nonverbal expression. At once, I started to research and develop methods for using intermodal learning in my special field of work. The first reactions of my students were very positive and encouraged me to continue my research. I took up the course *Education as an Art* at ISIS in Zurich, which gave me the basis for the method of intermodal learning. In addition, the Independent Study Degree Program at Lesley College gave me the frame and the support to transfer the intermodal method to my special field. The result of my research and my studies is the present book, which is a revised form of my master thesis. To write my thesis and the book in a foreign language was a big challenge for me. I found this to be somewhat of an analogy to the children whose challenge it is to learn and to reach the learning goals in a nearly unknown foreign language within an unknown culture. Out of my situation, out of my reactions, either positive or not, I now feel myself closer to my students.

The method of intermodal learning corresponds to my way of thinking, feeling, and acting, especially toward multiculturalism and education. The method helps to develop the personal and the social as well as the cognitive competence besides learning the new language. It is a resource orientated method based on the natural effort of development and strengths of each student.

My multicultural position is based on the understanding I have gained in looking at many personal stories of children in my multicultural class. And through all the years, my point of view has changed. In the beginning, I emphasized the child's origin, his or her mother tongue and religion. I tried to make links to the culture of the home countries of the children. But this often ended in clichés, which didn't belong to the child's world. As an example

> a twelve years old girl from Sri Lanka asked me if she could bring music from Sri Lanka to school to listen to. I was very pleased thinking of hearing sitar music or another original sound, but what I got to listen to was Michael Jackson.

My background also stems from reflections on the fascism in the Second World War, from reflections on religious and ethnic wars, from reflections of fundamentalist groups and sects in Switzerland, and finally from my reflections on the war in the former Yugoslavia and Bosnia-Herzegovina and my working experience in that country shortly after the war. As we have seen so many times, self-confidence which is only based on belonging to a fundamentalist collective, or to an ethnic or religious group, is dangerous for humanity.

In the summer of 1997, I left school to concentrate my work on in-service training, supervision, counseling, and school-development projects. Further, I'm involved in the coordination and implementation of bilingual educational programs for children from Kosovo, living in the Canton of Zurich. Especially for traumatized children, who have experienced war and crimes, the development of the ability to express themselves is a fundamental task with a high priority. I hope that this book will be an appropriate and useful contribution to education, especially for children with special needs.

Zurich, September 1999

# Chapter 1

# Children with Foreign Mother Tongues

## Context

### Quotations

School is a place of human education for the rising generation.

Joy should be the prevailing mood of the school.

School is not only preparation for life in the future; but it is a part of actual life to be formed.

Ten basic attitudes mark our school:

- Searching for orientation and insight.
- Responsibility.
- Achievement for learning and ability.
- Solidarity and dialogical communication.
- Tradition consciousness.
- Ecological awareness.
- Competence for critical thinking and to form an opinion.
- Creativity and cultural participation.
- Open-mindedness.
- *Leisure.* [2]

(Curriculum for compulsory education of the Canton of Zurich, 1991, pp. 3–5; translation by the author)

My field of teaching and research: A special integration class for non-German-speaking immigrant children called *Kleinklasse E*; a primary school (Grades 1–6) with 18 classes and about 240 students; a school where the mother tongue of about 93% of the students is not German (our school district: 75%; the city of Zurich: 40%; the canton of Zurich: 23%); a school where the children are speaking a variety of more than forty different languages at home; a school in a very underprivileged district of the city; a school which therefore has some privileges, e.g., a regular class shouldn't have more than 18 students (regular limit: 26 students).

The integration class *Kleinklasse E* is for non-German-speaking newcomers who are older than first grade students. First grade students normally start school in a regular class accompanied by a German language course. An integration class shouldn't have more than twelve students. The goal of the integration class is the integration of the students into regular classes as fast as possible. The approximate length of attendance is one year, but it may last a shorter or longer time, depending on the individual situation. Therefore, students enter and leave the class during the school year.

**Good Bye**

Friday afternoon before winter vacation.
The last day of school for Alissa.
She is moving to another town
in the French part of Switzerland.

"Alissa, please go out into the hallway for a minute."

Jathursa hides a little present,
a box of colored pencils, behind the curtains.

"Come in, Alissa."

Alissa starts to search for her present.
The class and Alissa know about the rules of this *say-good-bye* ritual.
When Alissa turns to a wrong direction, the children shout "cold."
When she turns towards the hiding-place, they shout "warm."

Alissa stays in front of the curtain.
"Hot, hot, hot!"
She looks behind the curtain.
There it is.
Alissa looks happy and sad at the same time.

**Welcome**

Monday morning, three weeks later.
The children are writing sentences into their books.
It's quiet in the classroom.

Suddenly, someone is knocking at the door.
I open the door.
"Good morning. We would like to bring our daughter to your class."
The heads of the children turn to the door.
"A new student. A girl."
"Please, come in and have a seat."

The parents hand over the pink registration form.
I look at it.
Carmena, eight years old, from Brazil.
"Welcome, Carmena!"

"Children, this is Carmena.
She comes from Brazil.
It's too bad, that no-one speaks Portuguese!"
"Mrs. Hösli, I can speak Portuguese."
"But, Isabel, your mother tongue is Spanish."
"Yes, but I learned Portuguese by playing with my neighbors."

Isabel shows Carmena where to hang her coat,

"Bye-bye, Alissa."
"Bye-bye, friends."

"Mrs. Hösli, will the children forget
me now?"
"I won't forget you, Alissa."

"Bye-bye, Alissa. Farewell!"

the girls bathroom,
and her desk and chair,
which have been waiting for her.

"Bye-bye, Mom.
Bye-bye, Dad.
I'll see you in three hours!"

Ohlsen (1994) from the Department of Education describes the educational tasks of an integration class as follows: "To welcome the children; to give confidence; to create a good atmosphere of learning; to increase the students' self-confidence; to familiarize the children with the new surroundings; to introduce into local norms and customs; to educate towards tolerance; to support the living and learning together within a class whose membership is subject to frequent change; to develop contact with the parents; to inform the parents; to introduce the German language; to catch up on gaps in one's knowledge in other subjects, specifically in mathematics" (p. 14; translation by the author). Besides these tasks, the schedule and the program of an integration class are subordinated to the official curriculum.

I would like to describe the last class I was teaching in the school year 1996/1997. Another teacher and I have been sharing the job of leading the class. I taught 16 out of 28 lessons which included all subjects except swimming. Seventeen students attended our class, either all or part of the year: Alissa, Ayonna, Carmena, Dobrinka, Hasan, Isabel, Ismail, Jananij, Jathursa, Latifa, Leyla, Manuel, Mariana, Nuran, Rafael, Sarujan, and Sonia.[3] They came from eleven different countries: Brazil, Bulgaria, Dominican Republic, Kosovo,[4] Morocco, Portugal, Spain, Sri Lanka, Turkey, Yugoslavia, and Zaire;[5] and four continents: Africa, America, Asia, and Europe; and they spoke nine different languages: Albanian, Bulgarian, French, Kurdish, Portuguese, Serbian, Spanish, Tamil, and Turkish. They were seven to eleven years old, and they entered our class between September 1995 and June 1997. Two students changed to regular classes in October 1996, one went back to her home country in January 1997, and one moved to another city in February 1997. Two students had not attended school in their home countries and entered our class totally untrained. Five more students had to become literate in our alphabet. They were trained more or less in Tamil or Arabic scripts. At the age level of our students the school system of the Canton of Zurich allows us to teach in half-class groups during eighteen lessons a week. During these lessons the other students are attending classes in handicrafts, or are staying in a day care center or at home. The half-class lessons allow a more differentiated way of teaching and learning with the concentration on language and mathematics. According to the heterogeneity of the class, we developed two to four levels in language and two to six levels in mathematics.

The described situation of that school year represents an average situation. In 1993, I started to apply the method of intermodal learning in the subjects of German language, music, and arts. During my studies I extended the intermodal learning method of teaching and collected data for this book.

## Basic Conditions

The basic conditions are given by the curriculum for the compulsory school of the Canton of Zurich (1991), and by the recommendations according integration of immigrants, published by the Department of Education of the Canton of Zurich in 1995. In the Canton of Zurich it is a normal fact that children with a variety of cultural, linguistic, religious, and social backgrounds are living and learning together. Most of these non-German speakers are children from working immigrants of the second or third generation, a much smaller group of students are children of refugees or persons seeking political asylum. The Department of Education of the Canton of Zurich writes (Der Erziehungsrat des Kantons Zürich, 1995): "On one hand, minorities can be an enrichment; on the other hand, living together often doesn't take place without conflict. Society and school as well as all people who are living here have the task of learning to live together in a meaningful way" (p. 3; translation by the author).

The task of our school is to support each child according to his or her preconditions and according to his or her possibilities. That demand requires an education through classes that have a unifying as well as a differentiating and individualizing effect. Therefore, the curriculum asks for an integral assessment of each student where different preconditions (among them non-German mother tongue or multilingualism; arrival from a different school system) have to be taken into account. Further, it requires a variety of educational methods in accordance with the goals, contents, themes, and the students. Teachers themselves are responsible for the choice of the method. They are free to choose any method as long as it doesn't contradict the didactic principles and requirements of the curriculum. The curriculum is mainly orientated toward the ability to act. It asks for teaching by example. Elementary as well as high school should fulfill the requirement of respectable elementary and integral education for all, which should be a basis for further education and specialization after the compulsory school attendance of nine years.

## Multiculturalism and Education

**How many languages are there in the world?**
Mother,
how many languages are there in the world?
About six billion, dear child.
Mother, how many people live in the world?
About six billion, dear child.
As many languages as there are people?
But the two of us speak the same language!
Well, dear child, we use the same words.
But your story is not my story.

When I started to work with immigrant children in 1983, the intercultural section of the Department of Education in Zurich was very new. The discussion about interculturalism was in its infancy. The institutionalized discussion and research on this topic was an ongoing process which went through different phases. The ideas and ideals continue to develop and change. There are an increasing number of children from countries and cultures very far away from here. The sociocultural structure of our school is subject to continuous change. The search for optimal solutions and forms of schooling are ongoing.

The following stories of two children and the questions regarding their thoughts and actions reflect the core ideas of education in a multicultural society.

> A child, during the first week of the kindergarten, refused to draw a picture of herself. The teacher just couldn't find a way to motivate the child to fulfill that task. What was going on? What could be the reason why the child refused to draw herself?
>
> A second child was asking the teacher, after a swimming lesson while walking back to school under a heavy rain: "What are insects doing when rain is falling? And what happens when all the holes and hiding-places are occupied? What are the rest of the insects going to do?"

Now my questions about both children: What are their nationalities? Are they boys or girls? To what kind of religion do they belong? What kind of skin do they have? What is the language of each child? How old are they? What is the motivation for their actions? You as a reader can guess, you can find answers, you can easily find interpretations. Give yourself a couple of minutes to reflect on these two examples and the questions.

The first child is the youngest girl of a well-educated Swiss family who is living in a village up in the mountains. At home, the family speaks Swiss German, the spoken language in the kindergarten is Romance. The girl understood the task quite well, but she needed more time and didn't want to be embarrassed by a poor drawing. So she decided first to practice drawing herself at home. This is what her mother finally found out. The second child is just an interested and communicative child asking lots of questions of her teacher. She could be from everywhere in the world. She is seven years old, and she was living in Zaire (today called Democratic Republic of Congo) until a couple of weeks ago. Her advantage is that she speaks French, and my first foreign language (after High German) is French as well.

These two stories show that the motivation for doing, leaving, or refusing things are very individual and often hard to understand. These two children are just two examples of the whole range of personalities that make up our world, and I can only be aware of a very small part of their integrity. What does this mean for education in a multi-cultural context?

## First Goal: Integration of Variety

To support identity in a broad sense requires that religion and ethnic background be recognized as well as all other characteristics of one's identity. It can mean to be a child, a girl, a boy, a son, a daughter, a student, a friend, an enemy, sister, or brother; it can mean to be a member of a family, group, class, church, or social group; it can mean to have certain preferences, feelings, needs, ideas, interests, talents, weaknesses, longings, wishes, and visions; it can mean to carry out certain tasks and responsibilities; it can mean to wish to be alone, to be socialized, to be part of a group, to be successful, to gain acceptance and recognition; it can mean the desire to learn, to grow, to meet expectations, etc. It is a never ending list. And beside, every child has her or his individual and unique life story, his or her individual and unique context of life. Younger children get their identity through what they like or don't like, through what they can do, through what they own, through what they have done, through the people they love, especially through mother, father, sisters and brothers, and through the daily life at home.

Today children not only in our town but around the world are growing up in a pluralistic society. This means that many of different ways of life happen side by side; and different levels, social, political, and cultural levels, are involved. Alemann-Ghionda emphasized in a lecture given in Zurich in 1996 that linguistic and cultural variety should only be seen and evaluated as one facet of today's heterogeneity and complexity in school. Since many foreign children are coming from socially underprivileged families, concentration should be placed on supporting these children's special needs in learning. This means that every child should be considered to have a special need and that we must strive to meet these needs. In doing this social, individual, and cultural differences have to be taken into consideration. The integration of the variety should be natural. The differences shouldn't be emphasized; they should be recognized and appreciated as a natural fact. Schools are places where respect for different languages and ways of life should be gained. On the other hand, society has to make an important contribution. It has to adapt to the pluralistic world, by facilitating the immigrants' participation in the political life and responsibilities of citizenship and by facilitating naturalization, especially of young people.

## Second Goal: The Active Child as Part of the Community

When talking about the *Urhebertrieb* [*creative urge*] Buber (1995) refers to the fact that a human being likes to create things, and that children want to take part in the development of things. He emphasizes that the highest level of creativity would be the emerging of something which hasn't existed before through one's own intensively experienced action. The *Urhebertrieb* wants to do, but doesn't want to possess. Buber emphasizes the importance of the arousal of the *Urhebertrieb*. He thinks that this could be the way in which development of the human being can finally succeed. But to rouse the *Urhebertrieb* is not enough; it is only a precondition. In this phase a person is very lonely. At this point, education, in which relationship and dialogue are fundamental, has to start. Children have to be part of the group. They have to be educated to be part of the community, as creative human beings with strong personalities, which is able to go further than individuality or collectivism. And von Hentig (1996) postulates the importance of educating children and young people to develop the willingness for self-responsibility and responsibility within the community. Education which doesn't lead to political responsibility, which doesn't teach and qualify each individual to look after one's own role and responsibility within the community is not education.

**Third Goal: Bridging Identities through Playing and the Arts**

First of all a child is just a child; then a member of a family; then a child is settled in certain surroundings, in a certain context. The young child normally knows only very little of his or her native country. When children have moved to a foreign country where a foreign language is spoken, where the climate, the food, the customs are sometimes very different, their personal development enters a state of crisis. Added to this is the fact that many children were living with their grandmothers, aunts, or other relatives and barely know their immediate families. Gardner (1993a) describes the development of the interpersonal and the intrapersonal intelligences. He describes how the developing of each intelligence is connected with the other. Moving to another country provokes a great challenge in a child's interpersonal and intrapersonal development. A child needs time and help to manage this crisis in a good and successful way. Care of the child's personality is important. A child must have the chance to find a new identity in the new surroundings. At this time a child is very dependent. Therefore, most important are good relationships with the persons to whom a child relates most closely. These relationships have to be intense, authentic, emphatic, and responsive. It is especially important to take into consideration that immigrants and young persons belong to a highest risk group. Therefore, the needs of this group of young people must be met with the highest care.

During this crisis a child can easily find identity through his or her ethnic and religious roots. This is not wrong, but it can be dangerous for the child and the new community. To define one's self only by a collective attribute isn't enough. This would encourage racism. A child should now have time and space to find his or her personal roots, to become connected to their own *Urhebertrieb*. Working with art is a very helpful way for this to happen. A child creates what is important in the moment. Art gives space where a child has the possibility to develop whatever she or he likes. Art gives space where a child has the possibility to repeat primary experiences of early childhood, and where a child can gain new primary experiences in the new surroundings. This must happen on a material, emotional, and personal basis. Primary experiences facilitate language. Art gives space where a child has the possibility to connect the experiences of the new world with the experiences of the old world. It offers the chance to develop a new reality. Every child and every adult has to go through this process again and again throughout their lives, but a child in such a crisis needs much more attention and care and a safe space.

The following three examples of working with art at school illustrate the phenomenon of bridge-building to very personal earlier experiences. Such bridges may or may not occur. This is left to the child's inner guidance. At the same time these children had the opportunity of going back to the very beginning of their development of artistic expression to get in contact with their own *Urhebertrieb.*

> We worked several lessons with clay—First we just played with clay to relax and to gain knowledge of the material. The children constructed a lot of food, animals, faces, babies, volcanoes, stones, holes, and different structures. They experienced the clay with closed eyes. At the end Sarujan, a boy from Sri Lanka, made a *somosa*, a Tamil pastry. Two other girls from Sri Lanka got inspired and copied one of the pastries. The fourth child from Sri Lanka, Jathursa, followed her own inspiration and made a face. A girl from Zaire, Alissa, made a lot of sweets. She is a quite big girl and loves sweets. Rafael, a boy from the Dominican Republic, has been fascinated by volcanoes for a couple of weeks now. He wanted to make a volcano, but in the end he created a penguin that he liked very much. He told me that he liked his penguin because it was an animal of the water. A boy from Turkey, Hasan, made a square house (like houses in Turkey?).
>
> Another story—Latifa, a girl from Morocco, painted palms in expressive colors. Alissa from Zaire and Leyla from Kosovo got inspired by this theme. They started to paint palms, too. Alissa painted much more detailed and naturalistic palms. Leyla copied the colors from Latifa and painted palms which only slightly resembled palms. I guess that Leyla hadn't seen palms yet, but she is obviously a very interested child who looked ahead in this moment.
>
> And a third example—A Tamil girl who could hardly speak German was looking with me for a title for her collage. I presented to her a couple of German sentences which came to mind while looking at her collage. After offering about the tenth sentence to her, she finally looked at me with shining eyes and a laughing face—we had found the title.

In my opinion to look ahead, to progress, is very important and natural as well as looking back from time to time. I realized a long time ago that most children want to look ahead. Often, they refuse to look back. They have to determine for themselves the time to look back, to occupy themselves with the past, the native country, the rootlessness. So a matter of concern must be to strive ahead and at the same time offer space to build bridges to the past. Working with art in the intermodal method is a compelling way to fulfill this need.

The method of intermodal learning, where sharing is an important phase, is a good way to fulfill the demand of Buber (1995) for relationship and dialogue. Let's have a look at Rafael from the Dominican Republic.

**Photograph 1:** "The Bird Is Flying to Sri Lanka"

> After playing music to his volcano picture, he told us how happy he was. To play music reminded him of his father in the Dominican Republic. His father is a musician.
>
> And after Latifa, Alissa, and Leyla had painted the palm pictures, he told us about palms in the Dominican Republic.

## Teacher's Role in Reaching These Goals

As I have described, there is a need to give children space where they can look ahead as well back; where they can build bridges to their past; where they can develop their identities which include a positive relationship to their own culture, their own religion, their own families as well as to their own personalities. For this to happen teachers need to create an open-minded and global atmosphere at school where the teachers themselves are models. It must be an atmosphere wherein the children can recognize themselves in a natural and positive manner—in books, pictures, models, and in the teacher's attitude. It must be an atmosphere wherein variety is natural; it must be an atmosphere wherein dialogue and relationship are central.

Teachers have to be informed about the political, cultural, social, and working situations of the immigrant families. They have to be informed about the situation in the children's native countries. They have to have some knowledge about different cultures and religions. They have to be open to expose themselves to other cultures, for instance, by traveling or by learning a foreign language. School has to support the immigrant children to cultivate their mother tongue; and to cultivate their culture as long as it doesn't contradict our law or human rights; and they have to appreciate the natural effort of development of every person which is not dependent upon a country, a culture, or an educational level. This requires lessons which will meet, activate, and include the inner most feelings of a child.

Finally, teachers have to build bridges between school and family. Lanfranchi (1996) expounds on some interesting aspects. He mentions that knowledge of cultures and information on ethnic differences are important, and at the same time unimportant as well. Namely, first and central is the proper encounter. An encounter with a foreign person requires an encounter with oneself. He argues, that if we learn to know and accept foreign parts in ourselves through self-reflection and awareness of our own personality, we will be more qualified to work with foreign persons in a professional manner. Further, he postulates that every kind of psychological counseling is an inter-cultural counseling, because every human encounter is inter-cultural one. To be foreign does not start with the color of our passport, but starts behind our own threshold within our own homes and families.

Every encounter includes differences between people, and the results of an encounter depend on a variety of factors: sex, social level, social setting, religion, nationality, etc. Previous knowledge of cultures and information about ethnic differences can help to order impressions, to assimilate, and to form hypotheses. Important conditions for developing a dialogic and a cooperative relationship with parents are the acceptance of a variety of lifestyles and the knowledge and ability to deal with the phenomenon of inequality, aspects of which are the differences in social status and the balance of power. And professional dealing with differences means a tightrope walk between the awareness of differences and the stereotypes of such differences.

## Working with Immigrant Children

"I have something to say, but I do not know your language yet." A child, communicative by nature, equipped with the natural impetus to develop, has just arrived in a country and at a school where a language foreign to him or her is spoken. At least foreign in a verbal sense. The child is at the start of an important and complex phase of integration. He or she wants to be part of the group, to play a part in the class, to share, to communicate, and to learn. Many children share this situation.

In order to meet the child's essential need for communication, quick acquisition of the second language is important. But acquisition of the second language is only a part of the overall objective of integration, is only a part of the higher objective of a comprehensive education, as described by von Hentig (1996)—to strengthen human beings and to make things clear.

**Latifa**

Nine years old, from Morocco.
Her mother tongue: Arabic.
First foreign language: French (I can communicate with her quite well.)
Second foreign language: English (She only knows a few words.)
And now, the third foreign language: German.

Her first day in a Swiss class:

Latifa draws a tree with lots of red apples.
She draws flowers.
A dog kennel.
She draws clouds and the sun.

Latifa tells me what she has drawn.
"Would you like to know the meaning in German?"
"Yes."
And she wants to write it down too.
And she wants to learn to read it and to take it home.
Only later I realize that she cannot read our letters,
even though she has told me that she could.

Next lesson: Acting and guessing.
We act out things we see in the children's drawings.
And we guess what every child is acting like.
Acting and guessing—no problem for her.

My next instruction: Look for the most beautiful thing in your picture.
How does it sound? Which instrument goes best with it?
Latifa plays to every apple on her tree
a sound with a small xylophone.
Her apple tree with the red apples obviously became her score.

All musical works are recorded.
We listen to all musical works.
We paint all musical works.

Latifa mostly likes to draw to her own music,
and to the music Rafael has played to his sleeping volcano.

Initiation into a new language,
through her own pictures,
through visual language,
through body language,
through musical language,
together with the most advanced students,
together with Leyla, the other beginner.

Accepted by all.
Part of the whole.

According to von Hentig (1996), one criterion for the efficiency of education is the ability and the will to communicate. Therefore, language is imperative. However, for a student who does not yet know our language, he is deprived of this element, at least on a verbal level. On the other hand we notice that children who speak in different languages quickly meet each other in playing, in social exchange. They utilize nonverbal language in a very natural way.

Primary and almost the only types of communication and expression in education, at school during lessons, are the everyday languages and the scientific languages. Other kinds of expression, e.g., all artistic forms of expression and play, are normally of secondary importance. Wanzenried (1996) complements in his concept of *The Four Languages* the everyday languages and the scientific languages with the *languages of art* and the *languages of contemplation*. I will describe this concept in chapter 2.

In second language acquisition, the integration of the *languages of art* is very valuable and helpful. The extension of the forms of expression and representation in multicultural classes (and as well as in other classes and educational settings) is very beneficial: Unpronounceable things are made visible, stories are told, dialogs are created, personal interests become apparent, community is experienced, and new primary experience takes place through music, image, design, illustration, movement, and dance, as we have seen in Latifa's example. Intermodal learning is a good method for working with immigrant children. It offers an excellent opportunity for giving children, like Latifa, space for expression, articulation, communication, initiation, participation, illustration, and reflection, instead of being mute.

Dobrinka, a girl from Bulgaria, took this opportunity on her very first day in our school. It was the day we finished our half-year mask project. She could not verbally communicate with anyone including me. By using gestures, she asked for Ayonna's mask, put some towels on, went on stage, and presented herself: "Look at me, I have something to say!" And we looked at her, saw her, and applauded; and through this opportunity, she became part of the class.

**Photograph 2:** Dobrinka on Her First Day, with Ayonna's Mask on the Stage.

## Chapter 2

# Intermodal Learning

To begin, let's have a look within the classroom, where Rafael is learning with eleven other students:

**Rafael**

Nine years old, from the Dominican Republic.
He has been in Switzerland for nine months.
Tall and strong.
Even in the first minute
he gave me the impression of being very tense,
like a pressure cooker about to explode.
Full of anxiety and fear of making mistakes?

Last February, I wrote:
Doesn't communicate in German even after 2 1/2 months;
is unreachable, allowing no connection between him and us.
His painting is restrained,
and it seems as though he is not in contact with his roots.
What does he have to tell us?
Is my working method incompatible with his disposition?

My developmental desire for him:
Recover a relation with his own images and stories.

Often we've been quarreling and struggling for power.
I didn't feel good about it—he probably didn't feel good either.

Then last September we began working with clay.
Free experiments, free playing:
Knocking, tapping, beating, pounding, forming, folding, rolling, kneading . . .
Modeling with closed eyes:
Rafael gets a delicate and tender expression.
Beside him, Ismail is singing an Albanian song very softly.

The following Friday:
Rafael's piece of clay turns into a volcano.
Modestly, some clay balls spew out of the volcano.
Manuel copies the volcano. From his volcano, lava flows like water.
A man cries for help, runs away.
Rafael's volcano falls silent and disappears under the towel.
"Too bad, we have to stop now," he says.
"When will we play again with clay?"

Following two weeks of vacation.
"Do you remember the Friday before vacation?" I ask.
Immediately, Rafael remembers his volcano.
"Would you like to paint today?"
The children agree with enthusiasm.
My instruction: "Paint, whatever you like to paint."

I cannot give further help now.
Latifa and Leyla with their parents are knocking on our door.
Two new students for our class. Now, they need my help and my time.
So, the children start to work by themselves.

And what appears on Rafael's paper?
A volcano, a sleeping volcano, as he later writes.

Next day: All the pictures are hanging on the black board.
A dialogue takes place between Rafael and Ismail:
Rafael: "What did you paint?"
Ismail: "Beautiful colors."
Rafael: "Why?"
Ismail: "Because I like them. And what did you paint?"
Rafael: "A volcano."
Ismail: "Why did you paint a volcano?"
Rafael: "Because I'm interested in it."

I bring books and pictures of volcanoes and pieces of lava.
I tell about the existence of dead, sleeping and active volcanoes.
Rafael writes about his volcano:
*I painted a sleeping volcano. I like it.*

Next step: "Look for the most beautiful thing in your picture?
How does it sound? Which instrument goes best with it?"
Rafael plays to his sleeping volcano with high concentration
and in a very delicate manner on the xylophone.
And he sings softly the text he has written about the volcano.

I'm shivering:
Would I be able to meet my own inner volcano in such a loving way?

We listen to all musical work.
We paint all musical work.
While listening to his own music, Rafael is again painting a volcano.
This time, red "Z's" are floating out of the crater.
"My volcano is snoring," Rafael says.

Back to the clay.
Forming a work, which can be dried and baked.
Rafael wants to form a volcano.
With love and patience he is modeling and forming;
rapt, and with endurance.
He barely has enough time.
But at least, he is showing me his work:
A wonderful penguin.
I am surprised.
Rafael explains: "I love penguins because they love the water."

A fiery thing wanted to be formed, an aquatic animal appeared.
Balance of elements?
Since then, Rafael seems to me to be more calm and content.
Our relationship has obviously eased.

When working with art, Rafael is very present and alert,
and he is working and cooperating with intensity and seriousness.
He faces the challenges. He tries, searches, and finds.

This is an example of what an intermodal working process can look like. The process is as important as the product. The core of education with the intermodal learning method is the natural use of the different art disciplines of visual art, music, dance, literature, and theater. And within this context, working with art means much more than using art for a pleasant change, for regeneration, or enrichment of lessons. It means to find and offer the art disciplines which help people to better express their own themes; or to approach, meet, and become acquainted with unknown themes (Knill et al., 1995; Hösli & Wanzenried, 1997).

## Aspects and Phases of Intermodal Learning

An intermodal process includes different aspects and phases. Figure 1 shows these aspects and phases and the correlation between work and process.

**Figure 1:** Aspects and Phases of Intermodal Learning (Wanzenried, 1996).

The aspects and phases of an intermodal process are not subject of a particular sequence. They are alternated as required and are then introduced by the teacher, or they take place as logical results of the process itself. To clarify this, I will compare the different aspects and phases of intermodal learning with Rafael's working process. Within that process we can identify all aspects and phases of an intermodal process.

### Concentration: I am aware; I am ready

This phase may be quite short but can also be longer. We can recognize that aspect, i.e., as Rafael was modeling with his eyes closed; or after my question: "Do you remember last Friday before vacation?"; after the instruction: "Paint, whatever you would like to paint"; before playing on the xylophone, as he took deep breaths; as we were looking at all the pictures hanging on the blackboard; as we were listening to the musical work.

### Playing: I explore; I let it happen

We can best find this phase when Rafael was playing with the clay. Further, as Rafael was searching for the best instrument: He searched and tried different instruments for about half an hour, until he found the xylophone.

### Decision making: I recognize; I name it

At some point in time Rafael decided to form a penguin instead of the volcano. I can imagine that this decision was an intuitive and unconscious one. After a long period of exploration with different instruments, he decided on the xylophone. Obviously he demands a high standard of himself: The sound and the kind of instrument to play had to go with his volcano a hundred percent. He didn't search for an arbitrary solution. During that phase, I was in an intense dialogue with him. I helped him in searching for the best instrument. By the way, that intense search, that research for a precise and clear expression, carries out the demand for an extensive and comprehensive education. Rafael practiced in an exemplary way qualities he can apply in many ways, at school as well as in his daily life, in Spanish as well as in German.

### Shaping: I repeat; I crystallize

Playing with clay has been repeated several times. In a narrative way, I brought up earlier events so he could get in contact again and again with his volcano, and develop and crystallize his subject. He learned that his volcano was a sleeping volcano. Because of his picture and through the discussion with Ismail, I realized his interest in volcanoes. Now I was able to help him and the other children extend their knowledge.

### Presentation: I share; I perform

While working and playing with clay, the children were in continuous dialogue about their work, with each other and with me. They presented what they modeled, they showed their work, they tried to copy, they got inspired. To hang the pictures on the wall, to look at them, and to talk about them was another important event within this phase, as well as to play music about the pictures.

### Feedback: I accept; I release

An important phase. The dialogue between Rafael and Ismail represents this aspect in a impressive way. Further, every child gained knowledge as they painted new pictures to each musical work.

These are all individual processes. However, as Wygotski (1974) posited, deriving meaning is a process of social construction. It is in this phase where children concentrate while being part of a larger group, play together, make group decisions, shape ideas with input from others, present their work in a social situation, and provide feedback for each other, that they derive meaning and knowledge richer than the individual input, yet honoring each input.

## Important Principles of Intermodal Learning in Education

### Intermodal Transfer

An important methodical principle of the intermodal method is the intermodal transfer—the shifting from one art form, from one modality, to another. In the process with Rafael, we can see shifts from modeling with clay to painting, further to writing, to music, to painting again, and back to modeling. An intermodal process has at least one shift. The intermodal transfer extends experiences and broadens the meaning of a subject. For example, Rafael learned that his volcano would be a sleeping and snoring one. He learned that his volcano needed soft music that sounded like a lullaby. And as he formed a penguin instead of a volcano, he eventually found in an intuitive and unconscious way the opposite of the element of fire. Perhaps he experienced wholeness at this point of the process. But this is only a guess.

### Dialogical Principle

Applying the intermodal method means creating a community consisting of all the participating students and the teachers. The intermodal method calls for a dialogical education. (See also p. 78.) Dialogical education means developing a special relationship between the self and others. It's a relationship which exists as a difference between individuals who are unequal because of their role, but equal because they are human beings. All students and teachers are both learners as well as teaching persons through the mutual and reciprocal process of giving and taking. There are dialogues between students and teachers, between students and students, and between teachers and teachers. But there exists also the self-dialogue and dialogues between the students and their work. This self-dialogue is very important, especially for children whose knowledge of the main language is still very limited. It prevents them from becoming totally mute and enables them to be creative and active. Self-dialogue is an important factor and tool for teachers as well. Again and again, they have to make decisions in relation to the process, to lead or to let go, to stop or to continue, etc. An intermodal process cannot be carried out as a fully planned class. Teachers have to plan an intermodal process as a director plans a stage play. They have to have a kind of presentiment of the whole work and its process. They have to have concrete ideas of modules which can become part of the process. They have to decide about the next step; they have to prepare materials; and they have to set the necessary frames. They are responsible for the whole process. For teachers, these requirements call for constant awareness of both the ongoing process and of themselves. And it requires clear and professional decisions.

## Repetitious Principle

According to Bollnow (1987) competence and practice are correlated and cannot be separated. Competence is retained through constant practice. Practice doesn't start in the very beginning. It is always based on a certain competence which already exists in a specific manner. Through exercise the competence should reach a more complete state; however, it actually always remains an incomplete one. To practice in a good way means to progress. Bollnow (1987) writes that in comparison to animals, human beings are born with only very few essential life functions. They have to learn them first and have to exercise them through ongoing and patient repetition, until they reach familiarity. Therefore, practice and repetition are characteristics which naturally belong to human life. When talking about the quality of exercise, Bollnow (1987) distinguishes between exercising and a learning drill (p. 12). By referring to the exercising tradition of Japan, mainly the exercising tradition of Zen Buddhism, he emphasizes that to exercise should mean developing and knowing one's innermost self.

Repetitions within intermodal learning make sense. Repetitions provide the opportunity for continuing a process and to practice, deepen, and stabilize acquired skills. To start on a quite familiar point or with a familiar method helps the children explore and extend into new areas. Security helps them to search and to proceed. Security helps them in dealing with insecurity. Nevertheless, every practice needs a certain challenge, an incentive for learning. Besides repetition, simplicity and working in small steps lead to the successful application of intermodal learning.

## The Meaning of Structures and Frames

Every art discipline has its typical character with certain given conditions, which gives and asks for special frames. Every frame restricts and provides security at the same time. A frame can lead someone to a deeper experience; but a frame can be very painful as well. To set a frame is always a tightrope walk. Every frame has to be set very carefully by the teacher. The teacher is responsible for the process, for the respect of the artists and the their work. Setting frames is one of the most important preconditions for a successful process. It is helpful to set frames in a ritualistic manner. I have noticed that children will acclimate themselves quite easy and willingly to ritual-orientated frames. They love these kinds of repetitions. Frames given in a clear and ritualistic way seem to give the children confidence and security. To set a frame in a ritualistic manner means to always set the temporal frame within a discipline in the same way (e.g., with a bell during mask performing, music presentation, when moving, etc.).

The following table, divided into five aspects of intermodal learning, will help to select, reflect, and carefully set the appropriate structure and frame. I have chosen the form of questioning, knowing that every context, every group, and every process are different from each other. The suggested questions should help you think about your own questions whenever and wherever needed.

**Table 1:** Frames in Intermodal Learning

| | **How to set frames in an intermodal process** |
|---|---|
| ritual | For example:<br>• How to begin and end the lesson, the performance? By a sign? After falling silent? All together?<br>• Is there an audience? Are there listeners?<br>• If there is an audience, how will the actors enter and exit? How is the stage area and the audience area marked?<br>• Which rules are given for sharing and giving feedback?<br>• What happens with the work created? |
| social | For example:<br>• Should the participants work or act alone or in groups?<br>• Silently or in communication?<br>• With or without contact and/or in touch? |
| spatial | For example:<br>• When painting or drawing, what's the size of the sheet? When acting, where is the stage, and where is the audience? If their is no stage available, a stage room should be clearly marked.<br>• When exploring with music, do I need a second room? |
| temporal | For example:<br>• When moving or acting, how long should the performance take? Should the temporal frame be set by an instrument, by the teacher's voice, by agreement?<br>• When exploring with musical instruments, could the frame be set by an optical sign such as the lights? |
| material | For example:<br>• When painting or drawing, should there be a limitation of techniques or colors?<br>• When working with musical instruments, should I offer all instruments or only rhythmical or melodical ones?<br>• Should the protagonists go on stage with or without objects? With one or more objects? With or without costumes? With or without masks? |

## Construction of Realities in *Four Languages*

With language we can classify, we can move to higher orders of thinking and learning. With language we try out what we think. With language we objectify subjective experience to examine, analyze, and share with others. With language we create metaphors which enable us to broaden our experience and perception. In our culture, the verbal expression, written and oral, plays an important role. Communication at school, at work, at home, etc., happens mainly in everyday languages as well as in technical terminologies. The form and type of communication is dependent on the context. At school a student uses a different vocabulary than on the playground, on the street, or in the family. Further, there is a need for another kind of expression than the verbal one (e.g., artistic expression as in movies, theater, dance, literature, etc.; the contemplation with prayer; meditation; the quiet communication with the nature) where things beyond verbal expression can be expressed or communicated. These forms of expression and communication are normally of secondary importance in school. Wanzenried (1996) in his concept of *The Four Languages* complements the everyday and scientific languages with the *languages of art* and the *languages of contemplation*:

**Language Creates Realities**

Choose common everyday language
As you talk at home
In simple usual words
So we can find trust.

Choose language of explication
As science requires
In precise, unambiguous terms
So we can find definition.

Choose language of understanding
As arts allow us
In strong visual metaphors
So we can find meaningful communion.

Choose language of silence
As spiritual meditations
In awe and wondering questions
So we can find eternity.

Peter Wanzenried (1996)
(Translation by Decurtins, Hösli, Sherman, and Wanzenried.)

**Table 2:** The *Four Languages* According to Wanzenried (1996)

| Perspectives of Realities: The *Four Languages* | | | |
|---|---|---|---|
| **Languages of Art** | **Everyday Languages** | **Scientific Languages** | **Contemplative Languages** |
| Intuitive understanding with personal involvement | Pragmatic operations | Understanding and explication in an overview and from distance | Bearing of uncertainty and contradiction |
| • To look from a new point of view, from a different perspective of awareness.<br>• Playful and artistic expression.<br>• Re-construction and transfer into other modalities.<br>• Crystallized and formed statements.<br>• Expressing of unpronounceable things. | • Everyday theories control perception and interpretation.<br>• Commonsense and everyday languages in their different codes.<br>• Consistent attitudes for everyday practice and operational routine. | • Systematic observations and phenomenological reflections.<br>• Empirical examination and hermeneutic interpretation.<br>• Typologies, models and theories, paradigms. | • Getting quiet and attentive.<br>• Keeping questions unanswered; amazement; risking dialogues; praying, meditation.<br>• Paradoxes and parables as statements. |

The term *language*, used in this way is not meant in a strictly analytical way. It is used in the sense of an everyday metaphor and means models of representation, forms of expression, nonverbal mediums of communication to perceive and represent realities. For example, the term *water* can be expressed and understood in very different forms that all represent specific aspects of reality of the same element: e.g., water as a thirst quencher (everyday language); water as $H_2O$ (technical terminology); water as elixir of life (poetic language); water as a painting of a bubbling fountain (visual language); water as a virtual sequence of sounds (musical language); water as a symbol for purification (language of contemplation), etc. Approaching reality in different *languages* offers the advantage of finding different perspectives of reality, and leads to a more integral understanding. It is important to see the four different languages as connected, interwoven, and mutually dependent.

## Requirements for Significant Subjects

Today we know that learning is more effective when subjects are transmitted in an embedded context, i.e., the subjects need to be based on experience and action of the students to be significant enough to guarantee the learning achievement of every student. New learning methods call for meaningful subjects. But which subjects will be authentically meaningful for all, especially when students are coming from a wide variety of countries, cultures, and families? Which have the same preconditions?

**Truth**

"The earth is red,"
says the child in Malemchi Phul.

"The earth is ochre,"
says the child in Sienna.

"The earth is brown,"
says the child in Wermatswil.

"The earth is black,"
says the child on Mt Etna.

"The earth is marble,"
says the child from the marble beach.

"What's earth?"
asks the child in the city.

Intermodal learning facilitates to build bridges to the very personal story, to one's own world of experience, to primary experiences. It offers the children a chance to build bridges to what they experienced in their home countries, their former schools, their families. It enables them to express what is important to them, and to share it within their new community. Many past experiences are totally out of context in their new home, new city, and new school. It's a new environment with new norms and rules. Therefore, it's important for children to go through new primary experiences and to gain new ground together with all the other children in their class. To gain new ground is a significant subject itself for every child who has to find his bearings in a new environment. Further, this ground of shared experience involves itself in many subjects which are meaningful to the students. For example, Rafael expressed his interest for volcanoes, which later became a subject for the whole class. Rafael went through his learning process within a group of twelve children. Now, the children had a common experience to share. This is clearly recognizable within the dialogue between Rafael and Ismail:

Rafael: "What did you paint?"
Ismail: "Beautiful colors."
Rafael: "Why?"
Ismail: "Because I like them. And what did you paint?"
Rafael: "A volcano."
Ismail: "Why did you paint a volcano?"
Rafael: "Because I'm interested in it."

## Goals of Intermodal Learning

I will subordinate the goals of intermodal learning to the already introduced generic objective of education from von Hentig (1996), *to strengthen human beings and to make things clear*. Even I describe the two aspects *to strengthen human beings* and *to make things clear* as being equivalent. However, I initially concentrate on the first objective. Only after the basic needs, e.g., physical needs, needs for safety, belongingness and self-esteem, are fulfilled is one able to focus on learning in a relaxed and curious manner. On the other hand, positive learning experiences and progressive academic development help the student to achieve success and higher self-confidence, which further support the first matter of concern.

### To Strengthen Human Beings

One important goal of the intermodal method is the care for the well-being of each student. Moore (1994a) describes the importance of paying attention and taking into consideration the spiritual aspects of the everyday life and talks about the *care of the soul*. About the nature of the soul he writes: "It is impossible to define precisely what the soul is. . . . We know intuitively that soul has to do with genuineness and depth. . . . Soul is revealed in attachment, love, and community, as well as in retreat on behalf of inner communing and intimacy" (p. xi–xii). According to Moore (1994a) we care for the soul "by honoring its expressions, by giving it time and opportunity to reveal itself. . . . To the soul, memory is more important than planning, art more compelling than reason, and love more fulfilling than understanding" (p. 304). And further: "Fulfilling work, rewarding relationships, personal power, and relief from symptoms are all gifts of the soul" (p. xiii). On that basis, *care of the soul* means for me every smaller or greater action in one's everyday life which supports the well-being, the regeneration, the harmony, and the joy of a human being or a group of human beings, and which helps give identity and charisma. Particularly, every artistic and/or creative activity can support the care of the soul. With this matter of concern, the intermodal method is related to an old tradition. It has to be considered that since primeval times all over the world, humanity has resorted to religion as well as to play and to the arts for spiritual, mental, and emotional expression, to gain vision, especially in borderline situations. Specifically they utilized play, the arts, and contemplation to express unpronounceable, complex facts, and within recurring rituals, which gave the society and the individuals support and strength.

A further goal of intermodal learning is to support the identity, ego strength, and social competence. The intermodal method is a resource-orientated method, which serves the emotional and physical sensitization, and tries to bring out the genuine treasure of a learner. It builds on what already exists and on the individual strengths. It calls for personal things to be expressed. It refers to one's own subjects, and it shows and supports individual preferences and expressions. Art provides a vocabulary. In using art, children find their own *voices* with that vocabulary.

Intermodal learning promotes tolerance and social competence. The process fluctuates continuously between self-activity and interchange with the group and the teacher. During the process the student has to function within specific rules and frames (see p. 21). When looking at pictures, when playing music, when acting with masks, each student gets his or her own space for presentation. To get space, to have space, and to be protected at the same time is a very positive experience for all children. Through the process, the students learn that the variety of work and the subjectivity of beauty are natural facts. In this way, they experience tolerance. Here, the teacher's attitude is an important precondition and help to the learning process. Teachers have to be models by meeting the children and their work in a unbiased manner.

Another goal of the intermodal method is the address and support of a variety of preferences and intelligences. Gardner (1993a), within the theory of multiple intelligences (see also chapter 4), emphatically pleaded that, apart from linguistic intelligence and logical-mathematical intelligence, there is also musical intelligence, spatial intelligence, bodily-kinesthetic intelligence, as well as intrapersonal and interpersonal intelligences to be taken into consideration and to be supported. D. Sherman adds to Gardner's seven intelligences aesthetic intelligence and spiritual intelligence. The intermodal method fulfills that demand. It offers a broad spectrum of approaches and ways where learning and understanding can happen. It serves the needs of a variety of learning types, and helps the students develop a genuine understanding of a subject. Further, the method includes and integrates rationality as well as emotion.

### To Make Things Clear

A first goal is the extension of perception and sensory awareness, and the training of sensitivity as a precondition of cognitive development. Piaget (within Kegan, 1996) found that life passes in a continuing process of differentiation, i.e., from a more or less confused shape to a more subtly diversified and complex one. This happens through interactive processes with oneself and the people and things around us. Two examples will illustrate such processes: Ismail, a boy from Kosovo, painted for almost a year just *beautiful colors.* He played with colors, he experimented with colors, he put colors into sequences on his pictures in different modalities, etc. As he got to the task of expressing the opposites *loud and soft* as pictures, he chose for *loud* an expressive red; and for *soft* a very light yellow. The two pictures were recognized immediately by the other students. Once, as we were making masks of papier-mâché, Ismail and Rafael looked in the newspapers for colored pages to model a colored mask. I heard them discussing a color they found. Ismail called it blue; and Rafael called it purple. They asked me to judge. For me, it was definitely a bluish purple. Obviously, the two boys were in a process of gaining a more differentiated perception of colors. New vocabulary was necessary at that moment to establish the gained differentiation. These two examples show clearly that a creative process is accompanied by an intense cognitive process, specifically when the process happens within a group where sharing is possible.

The intermodal method helps students approach, meet, and become acquainted with uncommon things and situations, or familiar subjects can be consolidated. This goes for personal subjects as well as for subjects by which a student is challenged by others.

Last but not least, the support of the development of language is obviously one of the most important goals. There is an ongoing dialogue during an intermodal process, with oneself, with the community, and with the teachers. A child wants to know, to ask, to share, and wants to understand others. Dialogues and reflections on what was experienced and achieved take place. All these everyday conversations, which are often very short but arise directly from the interests of the child or the community, build an imperative basis for the development of the linguistic abilities. This goal will be discussed in chapter 3.

## Chapter 3

# Didactics within Multicultural Contexts

Creative action
in a safe environment,
in a new home,
in a new group,
stimulates growth
for it opens up
visibly, perceptibly
room
for new and uniting
stories.

What does the application of the intermodal method in the everyday life of a multicultural class look like? Views into three working processes which took place in my class are presented here to help you to further understand the principles of the intermodal method and to support the transfer of these principles to the practical work in the classroom.

The first example describes a mask project which lasted six months and took place during two lessons of music and art each week. While embedded in a larger common process, this project gives a student a good look at his/her individuality, his/her wishes and visions, his/her artistic abilities and preferences, and his/her inner impulses: "I show something which belongs to me!" Within the second example, the students deal with a subject introduced by me: The exploration of opposites. Before starting this project, I came to the conclusion that this was a subject with a deeper meaning to all, because every child has already met that universal principle during his/her life. In this process, the dialogue with others is an important tool for the individual learning processes, because: "Others should understand the things I express!" The process took place during several language lessons. The third example shows different intermodal activities which need to be seen as a whole. The students come in contact with works of famous and well-known artists and get inspired by their works and by the works of their peers: "I'm influenced by the world and my peers, and I have an influence on my peers and the world!"

## First Example: Mask Project

### The Beginning

Again and again I am fascinated by masks:
Expression.
People in motion.
Dance as an expression of the soul
emphasized by the mask.

What would be the reaction of the children?

Introduction through a mask book.
Through pictures of my own masks.
Through pictures, which show myself, getting a mask of plaster cast.

"Who will take the risk to get a mask of plaster cast?"
"Me, me,"—two voices.
"Me too, but without the eyes and the mouth,"—one voice.
"Not me, not me,"—again two voices.
And the others? Courage and fear, all together?

Let's start with Latifa. The others can help and watch how it's working.
A comfortable place to lay down.
An extra T-shirt to protect the clothes.
A hairband, vaseline for the skin, the small hairs, the eyes.
Gauze to protect the eyes, the mouth, the hairline.
One child has to hold Latifa's hand all the time.
One child can help me to lay small pieces of plaster cast on Latifa's face.

"Latifa, are you ready?" She nods with her head.
"No fear?" "No, not at all!" "OK, lets start."
Softly, carefully—two layers of plaster cast.
The other children: interested, calm, nervous, and helpful.

The mask is finished and has to dry for ten minutes.
Latifa is humming under her mask.
The children around her are singing Jingle bells.

Ten minutes are over. Latifa can sit up now.
She makes grimaces under the mask.

And slowly, slowly . . . "Hello, Latifa!"
Latifa looks at her mask as a mother is looking at her baby the very first time.
Latifa looks happy.

The list of volunteers to get a mask grew quickly to seven children.

## Short Sketch of the Mask Project

The mask project went on from January until June. Every Friday afternoon we worked for two hours during art lessons: Making masks of plaster to get models for papier-mâché masks; painting and forming of the masks; experiencing in movement, also during gymnastic lessons; finding fitting clothes; giving the mask a name; awakening ritual of the masks on the stage; going on stage six more times, alone, with and without an object, each time lasting 1–2 minutes; final performance with audience (parents and two classes of the same school); and final ritual: picture time and a say-goodbye ritual.

To clarify and to reflect on my work I interviewed two teachers of the same school, who attended the mask play. F., age 32, is a female fourth grade teacher. She attended the play during her spare time. M., age 33, is a remedial male teacher in a first grade class for children with special needs. He attended the performance with his students. The interviews took place in separate settings. The interviews had been given in Swiss German and then transcribed into German and English. I have organized this presentation of the interviews by subject matter. Still, the statements remain as authentic as possible.

## First Impressions

E: Ten days ago you and your students attended the mask play put on by my students. I am very interested in your thoughts about the play.

M: I liked the whole play very much. And I think it is a very good form for the students we have in our school district, and especially for the students you have in your class for learning our language. I think that it provides an excellent opportunity for them to express themselves through their strong points and resources they can use to compensate for their lack of a common language. And I appreciate the parents coming. A lot of them don't understand or speak German either. Nevertheless they could understand the play. All the children presented themselves as individuals, I mean as people. This was expressed in varied ways not only through their masks, but also through their clothes.

F: What touched me very much is the fact that I got the impression that every child created his/her own world on the stage. I mean really from their very own point of view. I don't know how it came about, but each mask was unique. Each child presented his/her own characteristics and within the five minutes of acting I got a picture of every personality.

E: Can you give me an example?

F: For example, the mask with the Chinese name somehow looked Chinese too: The way he stepped in front of the curtain and the way he bowed was very special. He was the clearest example for me, but all the masks were very special.

## Setting Frames (Theory see p. 21)

*a) To Follow the Masks' Individuality*

F: I remember the first mask. When she came on stage, she was crying. And she was filling the whole stage with her play. I'm wondering how it came about that every child could create his/her own world on stage. Is it a result of feedback given by children or by you? To what extent is the play the product of the group, or the product of each student individually?

E: I began in the same way we started the final performance. All the children were behind the closed curtain. I called the masks by their names when it was their turn to go on stage. There, they introduced themselves by bowing. Second, they crossed the stage by using different kinds of stepping forms. My advice was always: "Walk like the mask likes to walk. Ask your mask how to walk." In this way, they also decided on the clothes: "Ask your mask which clothes it prefers." In the beginning, the students were very shy, so, the third time, I gave the advice: "Let the mask play. Let the mask do something." And the mask you mentioned before, the crying mask—it happened like this: Maybe it was during the fourth entrance. In the middle of her play, she suddenly started to cry and pointed behind the curtain to an imagined bad child who had beaten her.

This was a very new scene, a new creation for her. So I told her, to repeat that scene. I emphasized that scene, so the scene became a part of her own repertory. Later, I asked her if she would like to start with that scene. By watching the children, I search to find the new creations in each student's play. I lead the students in this way.

F: And you hadn't the feeling of being too rigorous? Did they accept your instructions?

E: Yes, there was a structure which placed limitations on the acting. I was aware of that limitation and I had to deal with both sides. I didn't

**Photograph 3:** Miri, the Crying Mask

force a child, but I motivated them to continue and to repeat and to repeat until finally finding their own work. At the end, every child knew how to start the final performance, but the rest was up to them. I have found for myself that the result of that kind of limitation was clarity and depth.

F: I think that every performance was different—not different in their qualities but in their message. All scenes were deep and concentrated. And, another point—I'm astonished that the second part of each scene was unplanned. I had the impression that the scenes were played in one go, and all children would *lead their own brushes*. Yes, I was very impressed.

E: Do you think the statement that the masks were playing and not the children is true?

F: Yes, very much so. And I had the impression that at the same time the mask was a protection for the child. For example, the queen was really walking like a queen. I asked myself if the child could also walk in such a royal manner without a mask. Yes, it was really the mask leading the child.

E: I have an example which probably supports that theory: We did a say-goodbye ritual. The children said goodbye to their masks before putting them under a cloth. A boy said: "Goodbye, Tschim," and added, "You played great."

**Photograph 4:** Queen Mitri

F: (laughed): So they experienced the play in the same way. They, and they and their masks, are something different.

*b) Alone on Stage*

M: I thought about your reasoning for sending the children on the stage alone rather than have them play in groups or perform dialogues. I felt, that was the form you decided on, and I saw that you applied it very consistently. I felt that this form is very fair. Each child has the same space at one's disposal. They don't have to fear rivalry. On the other hand, it places the child in a vulnerable situation. Your students seemed to react in different ways. Some of them definitely enjoyed it, some others found ways to somewhat hide—they acted on the edges of the stage or they copied things of others.

**Photograph 5:** Tschim's Performance with the Chair

E: I also see both aspects. At the end, I asked each child separately what they preferred: To act or to be in the audience. Only two children preferred the audience. One was the child who performed the brilliant scene with the chair. Further, I asked if they would like to continue acting on stage and they all wanted to.

M: Ah, super.

E: To send them on the stage alone is a methodical question. The students have to fulfill the mask's request. Second, there is the audience. And third, they had the possibility to also bring an object on the stage. I realize now that this third point was at too high a level for most of the children.

c) *The Sign of the Tibetan Bell*

M: I liked the fact that you marked the beginning and the ending of each scene with a sign. It was highly effective, and I am sure it was a big help for the children. I had the impression that most children needed your help. You had to know each child very well to find the right point of time for ending the scene together with the child.

E: I think that I gave the sign too early a couple of times.

M: Yes, once I had that impression too. But that's not so bad.

## Goals

a) *Development of Ego Strength, Identity, and Social Competence*

E: What do you think the children learned?

M: I think they learned a lot. They certainly learned how to get along with each other socially. They learned to show each other ideas, to stand by and say: "Look at me, that's me!" They learned to show weakness: "I'm afraid of this or that. This is hard for me." They showed their emotional faces, feelings, emotions, and images. And I think through this experience the personality grows socially, individually, and emotionally.

F: I also think they learned a lot. They learned to take space and be present with themselves: "Me and my mask are able to fill the stage. They are looking at me. They cannot hear me, but they are aware of me."—And then as you said before, by following the mask they learned to give attention to something, to a situation, or a fact. They had to bear stress like: "It's uncomfortable. I'm afraid." They had to bear feelings, pleasant and unpleasant ones. I think when forming the masks a lot of things happened. To let others make a mask onto one's own face is an exercise of trust. And to look at oneself, to have a vision, and to develop that vision: "It's not me, but it's a part of me." I am for sure they also learned a lot about the applied techniques. I think these are the most important facts.

E: After her performance, I asked the girl who played Queen Mitri: "What did you think while performing?" She answered: "I thought, if I make a mistake the others would laugh at me. Then I realized that I wouldn't die." Then I asked her, what she thought she had learned. Her answer was: "I learned that when I stopped being afraid it was fun, and that the others could enjoy it too."

F: Hey, that's great!

*b) Support of the Integration*

E: Can you see a benefit from this performance toward my task of supporting the integration of the children in their new environment?

F: Yes. I have the impression that taking space has a meaning for integration. Integration doesn't mean only to adapt. It also means to take space. Otherwise it's not possible to integrate oneself. On the other hand, integration also means to integrate a part of oneself, perhaps to integrate the part which was expressed by the mask.

M: My previous comments would apply to this question as well. I felt the performers saying: "I'm not only here with my words, I have different aspects. I show something, and the others are looking at me. I'm looking, and the others are showing." I mean, for me, the main purpose is the development of the personality. And there, integration is included.

F: I had the strong impression that every child was filling the room. I think that is why I'm touched so deeply. I would love to see every human being in this world fill his or her space in his or her own very way.

*c) Development of Language*

E: Do you see how this activity can benefit the learning of German as a second language?

M: Yes, I think that all which is experienced, which is gained by doing can be transferred into language. That's somehow the basis for language. I think, afterward this they can learn more easily the expressions for feelings, for situations, and for all things around the theater. And they won't forget these expressions, because they have been experienced.

E: Do you think that experience is the basis on which language develops?

M: Yes, but it doesn't happen so easily. You have to connect the experiences with the language. You have to talk about it after the event. You have to use the new expressions. If I were learning a new language, I could imagine that this experience would be a big help for me. I could imagine first to play a scene, without words, only with mime. And afterward, we could talk about it. I could concentrate on one thing at a time. I can imagine that after playing I could express myself in a better way. I could tell what the scene was about, what I did, what was first, what was second, what I felt, etc.

E: As a teacher, having seen the play would enable me to be even more helpful to my students.

M: Yes, because you know exactly what I'm talking about. I'm not just talking about my vacation in Greece where we have nothing in common. That's not like this. We have a common situation to share. This process would be a big help for me.

F: I think everything they experience and express, through telling, asking, etc., is cognitive learning as well, specifically for these children for whom the acquisition of a second language is important. The experiences are connected with language.

E: So you have the impression that this is a beneficial activity for learning a second language?

F: Yes, sure. I think the children experienced a lot and in a very deep way.

E: Even if language is excluded by wearing masks?

F: Yes, but language was excluded only within the last five minutes. During the whole process a lot of language happened. While shaping the masks, you were in dialogue. You talked about the techniques, about wishes, preferences, about rules, etc. And all these went over the German language. The children practiced language in a very embedded context.

E: I like your answers.

F: Yes, I just thought that perhaps my answers were not critical enough, but this is really my opinion. I like your work.

**Isabel**

"No, I don't want to do a mask of plaster; no, not at all."

Isabel has discussed the problem with her father.

"My father told me that I don't have to do it if I don't want to."

"That's right, Isabel. You can help, and if you want to do it later, that will be OK."

Isabel was present all the time by helping the others,
by holding hands, by washing the faces,
by putting plaster cast on faces.

Isabel, the only child without a mask.
Even Jananij had decided to make one.
Even the very newest child announced by gestures that she would like a mask.
Before the announcement she had been holding lots of hands.

I decided to talk again with Isabel.
"Would it be possible by leaving your mouth free?" "No."
"Would it be possible by leaving your eyes and your mouth free?" "No.
You know, I'm very much afraid. I was once in the hospital to get an injection
and four persons had to hold me."
"Do you want to lie down and we would start to cover only
the front, the cheeks and the chin?
And you decide yourself how far we cover your face?"
"Yes, That's a good idea."

Soon after we started:
"Mmh, I like it."
"Should we try to cover your eyes too?
If it's not comfortable for you, we can remove it quickly."
"Yes, please do it."
"Should we try to cover your mouth too?"
"No, definitely not. I want to be able to talk."

Ten minutes to let the mask dry.
Isabel is humming.
The children around her are singing Jingle bells.

Time to remove the mask.
"Hello, Isabel!"

"Mrs. Hösli, can you close the mask's mouth?"
And: "May I do another mask next Friday? It was fun!"

Isabel was happy to see her mask with a closed mouth like the others.

## Learning Effects on the Students

At the end of the process I asked each student individually: "What did you learn during the whole mask project?" Here are their answers:

"I learned that my mask wanted to sleep and to jump on the stage."

"I learned to play and to dance, and to cut with scissors and a knife. And I learned new words."

"I learned what the mask wanted: The right clothes, the right instrument, etc. I learned body language."

"I learned to not be afraid on the stage. I learned that the mask wanted to play with a string."

"I learned to make masks out of plaster. I learned to paint, and I learned German."

"I learned to act with my mask. I learned to paint."

"I learned that it is much better to bow two or three times in front of the curtain instead of only once."

"I learned to not be afraid on the stage. I learned to do a somersault on the chair."

"I learned to play with my mask on the stage. I learned to paint."

"I learned to act with my mask."

"I learned that I can have fun and make the other children laugh. I learned that the mask tells me what to do, like a *big mother* or like a computer in my head."

## Effects on Others

E: What was the reaction of your students?

M: We talked about it briefly, and their reactions were very positive. They really liked it, and some of them asked spontaneously if we could do the same project. And they remembered details. Once before I had gone to the theater with my students. There, the play went on too long. This play was just perfect for them. They could follow it very well.

E: They didn't get noisy?

M: No, no. The length was perfect, and they understood the play. They reacted with laughter, waving, etc., creating a dialogue of sorts.

E: What does that final performance mean for you?

M: I would like to do a project like this with my students. I haven't put on play for a long time. It encourages me to try something new.

E: What's the meaning of the final performance for you?

F: Once again I am reminded of the importance of beginning with what is here, what the children bring. For me this is a basic attitude, and I'm happy that you have reminded me of that attitude once again.

### The Finale

Friday after the final performance, the final ritual:
We sit on the floor, in a circle, around an orange towel.
The children say goodbye to their masks,

and put them under the towel.
"Goodbye Miri, Cimona, and Cima.
Goodbye Jin Huan, Kiridsha, and Queen Mitri.
Goodbye Nani, Tamilni, and Night Sky.
Goodbye Midu, and Bolo, sister of Pocahontas."
And I hear Ismail saying to his mask:
"Goodbye, Tschim, ciao, you played great."

The children take their masks home.
"Farewell!"

## Second Example: Opposites

It was during a normal German lesson when suddenly I hit upon the idea of implementing an intermodal process with the theme *opposites*. I was teaching opposite words with the advanced group in a quite structural way by pictures and by memory playing, when I realized that a new child in my class, Alissa, was silently repeating these opposite words. The girl was unacquainted with the German language except of a few words and short sentences. This happened during the time I was reading a book of von Hentig (1996). There he argues for choosing themes which will have major educational effects. And these should be themes, events, and methods, which are effective for *all* students. I began to think about the life principles of dualism, ambivalence, and aswellas. I drew the conclusion that the theme *opposite* would be such a theme with a deep effect for all students, if taught and experienced through an intermodal process. Besides new German expressions, the children should experience the phenomenon of dualism. They should gain comprehension for that kind of correlation. An understanding of such a principle can be gained in any language. I decided to start the intermodal process during the next German lesson with the group of the advanced students together with the group of the beginners.

### Alissa

Seven years old, from Zaire.
The youngest student in the class,
but full of vitality, full of questions, very mature for her age.
Her mother tongue is French.
This facilitates communication with me and also with Latifa from Morocco.

"What are the insects doing when it's raining? And what happens if all cracks and holes are taken?"

"Why has Sonia gone? After all it's normal that we all are homesick!"
"Why can't children experience deep friendship? You know, I would like to have a friend."
"Why do Swiss people dislike foreigners? I saw a discussion about that on TV."
"When I'm grown up, I would like to talk three languages: French, English, and Chinese.
You know, I would like to work as a physician in China."

A girl full of questions, a girl full of thoughts.
With me, Alissa is always speaking in French.
With the children, she is already speaking in broken German after only two months.
Soon, after the forthcoming birth of her sister, her family will move to Lausanne.
In a short time, she is accepted and integrated into the class.

Alissa is a very attentive and nosy girl.
I saw her taking part in the lessons for the advanced children from the background.
She was repeating silently the expressions I was teaching to them instead of doing her work.
She was obviously interested in that material.
Why not initiate an intermodal process on the principle of polarity and dualism with both groups?
The advanced together with the three beginners?

Opposites, expressed by movement.
Opposites, expressed by musical instruments.
Opposites, expressed by paintings.
A principle, which exists everywhere.
A principle, which can be experienced by all.

Alissa's choice was ambitious:
round and angular.
Her search was an intense one.
What she found was precise:
The drum beat for round,
the sound of strings of the psaltery for angular.

"I didn't choose the drum for *round*, because its shape is round.
No, I chose it because it sounds round.
And I chose the psaltery not because its shape is angular,
I chose it because I can play an *angular* sound on it."

Alissa was interested in the words we used.
Now she knows these words in a new language.
Perhaps they came as an extension in her mother tongue as well?

Through the senses we found deeper meaning.

## Sketch of the Subject of Opposites

Step one: Repetition of the words through a memory game. Expressing opposites by moving. Each child chose a pair of opposites to express with one or two instruments. Playing their music for the group; recording the music; listening to the music; and judging by the child and the group: "Does it fit?"

> First, Latifa was not satisfied with her music. Her word choices were *mad* and *kind*. She thought both parts of her music were *mad* music. The group agreed. So she looked for a new instrument and tried again to express *kindness*. The second time she was successful.

Step two: Listening to the recorded music; moving with the recorded music; painting the chosen and enacted opposites on the sectors of a large paper circle (see photographs 6 and 7).

> Sarujan had chosen *fast* and *slow*. It was easy for him moving fast and slowly. It was easy for him expressing *fast* and *slow* on the drum. And it was easy for him painting in a fast way a thick brown line on one segment, and with slow motions lots of yellow short lines on the other segment. But he seemed to me very puzzled as the other children deciphered the brown line as *slow* and in the short yellow lines as *fast*. Only after a girl was slowly following the brown line with her finger accompanied by the words: "I see a snail's track," could he understand the other point of view. In his yellow short line he suddenly saw fast rain drops. In the end he decided to name his two pictures as the others had seen them.

All the class learned about searching for common understanding: Are the others able to see what I see in the picture? Is my expression meaningful to other people? Is my expression a more or less reliable one? In this moment, the group itself became an important partnership for learning.

To reinforce the learning process, we repeated the task of painting a pair of opposites. This time we painted the *two sides of a coin*. To examine the results, the children had to guess the expressed opposites.

## Goals and Principles of Intermodal Learning

a) *The Choice of Modalities—self-interview.*[6]

K: Why did you start this intermodal process with moving rather than with another modality?

E: Children are normally very agile. A child has to jump, run, and move. I was teaching a beginner and an advanced group and, therefore, I decided to begin with a well-known modality. Other modalities like music and painting are not as common and naturally experienced as moving.

day

happy

sad

night

slow

soft

big

small

loud

fast

**Photograph 6:** Opposites I

slow fast

happy sad

**Photograph 7:** Opposites II

K: Next, you shifted from movement to music, and afterward to visual expression. Why did you decide on that order of intermodal transfers? I guess that painting is a more familiar discipline than musical expression.

E: Children are very fascinated by instruments, but only very rarely do they have a chance to play instruments themselves. So they are open to them. The task of expressing a pair of opposites with instruments was really a challenge. It offered an untouched, inexperienced, creative realm, wherein the students could develop something of their very own. All these factors supported my decision for that shift.

K: Nevertheless, next you shifted to visual expression.

E: To end the process I wanted the students to have permanent works to present, to compare, and to take home to share the experience with their parents. Music is a fleeting art discipline, and the crystallizing art at the end is something to see, to contact, to hang on the wall. It's like a symbol for the whole process.

K: Did they paint new things or did they reconstruct figures and pictures used during the introductory phase?

E: I was really impressed that they painted new things, real and symbolic ones. For example, to express *loud*, Ismail used an expressive red, and to express *soft*, he painted a very light pastel yellow. To express *happy*, Jathursa painted laughing people, but she expressed *sad* by symbolic raindrops.

K: Did the children find these symbols without your help?

E: Yes, they did. And for me, it was a logical consequence of the shifts in this intermodal process. Every intermodal process opens a door to deeper personal knowledge.

*b) Clarification*

K: Can you emphasize other important concepts which helped the children gain clear results, even though they are not skilled in painting or playing instruments?

E: It's important to develop sensitivity toward the theme and the modalities. This helps to clarify expression. Further, there is the dialogue between the children themselves and with me. For example, Sarujan wanted to express *slow* and *fast* by a drum. I encouraged him to clarify the two opposite speeds. He tried again. I encouraged him to try to get even more explicit. This was a difficult task for him, especially to keep the beats slow. Afterward we reviewed the musical expression by listening to the recorded sounds. The children gave feedback to their own and to the others' work. Whenever the result was not satisfactory, the children looked for a better form of expression.

K: Wasn't it too hard for the children?

E: I don't think so. A child likes to be challenged as long as the atmosphere and the relationship with me and their peers is good. At school it's quite normal to challenge a child in mathematics or in language. Why it shouldn't happen in art? One goal of intermodal working is the encouragement and support of the children.

K: I agree. Do you have a second example which shows a clarifying situation?

E: There was the examination of the painted opposites by students who didn't take part in the process—an examination by a *foreign glance*. The students had to assign the written adjectives to the painted expressions.

K: Did it work?

E: First and with determination they deciphered *loud* and *soft*, expressed in a rich red and in a pastel yellow. But they had difficulties with *happy* and *sad*. The students could decipher the gray raindrops as *sad*, but they couldn't find *happy*. Jathursa, the creator of these opposites, had painted laughing people, but none else could make out these laughing people in the red lines and spots. Her skills of figurative painting still were quite weak.

K: What was her reaction? Did she feel badly?

E: I don't know. We discussed her painting problem in the group. Other students told her how they would solve the problem. So Jathursa got a second piece of paper and started to paint again. This time she painted two girls with really laughing mouths, and she was successful. I had the impression that she was very proud of her final result.

### c) *Deep and Wide Learning Effect*

K: To get in contact with others, to be examined by a *foreign glance*, seems to arouse a deep learning effect.

E: Indeed, besides learning new expressions, experiencing opposites in different ways, trying to express invisible things through visual art, and expressing visual things by sound, the students were challenged in finding a common understanding in their expressions. Sarujan was really surprised that the others deciphered his two paintings the opposite way. When we repeated that task by painting the *two sides of a coin*, he turned to an easier pair of opposites. I had the impression that he really tried to express them in a way the others could recognize. In other words, Sarujan learned to look with a foreign glance to solve the task.

K: Sarujan got a second chance, and he obviously was successful. How was the reaction of others, e.g., of successful students. Didn't they get bored?

E: No. For example, Rafael was successful the first time. The second time, he searched for a pair of opposites we hadn't mentioned before. His choice was *black* and *white*. A couple of days before, the children learned the expression *secret*. It's quite a difficult expression to explain. Therefore I took the opportunity to apply that new word. The children's choice of opposites were to be kept secret. I knew their secrets so I could help the students whenever needed. At the end, we made an exposition with the painted opposites. And the students had to guess the correct words. Rafael was quite nervous about the reaction of the children. Would they understand him?

K: Did they? I think that *black* and *white* would be quite easy to understand.

E: Sure, but his challenge was finding and presenting something new. And it worked. I extended the expression of his coin by adding the words *bright* and *dark*, and *day* and *night*. This was a good example to show the children that symbols can be differently interpreted, and that other interpretations can be right as well. I had the impression that Rafael was ready for such a refined interpretation. He was surprised, but he looked happy to me.

K: It seems that you gave the students a chance to set their challenge themselves?

E: That's right. And this is a natural fact in children's lives. Children set their own goals from birth. They are repeating, exercising, or setting new challenges according to their actual needs and stages of development.

*d) The Position of Systematic Learning*

K: All the mentioned learning goals are also goals of your official curriculum. In addition, the students have to learn to read and to write with correct spelling; school has to measure, has to give grades. How do you handle this?

E: It's very important to fulfill all these requirements. For me, logical approaches and art orientated approaches go hand in hand; they are not inconsistent. It's always a tightrope walk to decide on one approach over another. It depends on the children's stage of development, on the actual situation, and on the learning subject.

K: This reminds me of the theories of Montessori and Piaget.

E: Yes, me too. Their theories are important in my work.

K: Can you give some examples of how you integrate the different goals?

E: I will give you two examples. First, besides the intermodal process, the students of the advanced group wrote the opposite words they had used. We built and wrote sentences with these words. Piaget emphasizes the importance of naming experienced things.

K: An intermodal shift into poetic language.

E: Yes. Then, they learned to read these sentences. They learned to write some of these sentences from memory. Second, in dialogues during the process, I realized that the majority of the group had problems interpreting interrogatives correctly. After finishing the intermodal process, the next theme was clarifying interrogatives. I have done this in a very systematic and direct way.

K: In other words, you try to connect art orientated learning and systematic learning.

E: Yes, during an intermodal process, where the dialogue is central, I try to find out what could be important to practice systematically, e.g., reading, writing, learning about sentence structure, tenses, to look at conjugation, etc.

K: You explained that cognitive learning and intermodal learning go hand in hand. Nevertheless, do you have a priority and why?

E: Yes, every student should learn in an embedded context. Cummins (1984) explains that clearly in the figure of a *dual iceberg* (see chapter 4). First and central for me are common experiences. These could be an intermodal process or encounters in nature, with people, with objects, etc. Learning by doing, exploring, and experiencing is important. It lays a basis for further learning.

## Third Example: Intermodal Learning

### Ismail

Ten years old, from Kosovo.
Shortly before Christmas, he came to our class,
directly from Kosovo, without knowing a word of German, totally untrained.
His anxiety was obvious.
He couldn't read or count,
but he was intrigued by the watercolors.
He started to paint, at a quite early childhood level,
without being ashamed, full of joy.
Immediately, he got in touch with his creativity.
When we made an exhibition
he proudly presented his pictures.

Nine months later, Ismail influences the class with his childlike naturalness:
He just paints colors: red, yellow, and orange.
A very dynamic picture.
As Rafael asks about his theme, he answers:
"I painted beautiful colors."
And as Rafael asks about the reason of painting just colors, he answers:
"Because I like them."
I admire his natural casualness.

He writes a short story to his picture.
I have to help him with the writing.
But step by step he gets more familiar with the letters.
On a kalimba—an African instrument—he plays a soft and warm sound to his colors.

After playing music to pictures or to objects in pictures,
we listen to *Peter and the Wolf* of Serge Prokofiew.
Ismail is very impressed that a man did the same as we have done:
He composed music to a story, to a picturebook, to persons, to animals.
And Ismail is able to recognize these persons and animals.
His eyes are shining when he hears the cat jumping on the tree.
Ismail takes the music home to listen to it again with his father and mother.

Other children start following Ismail's example of painting beautiful colors.
After we've been looking at pictures of a variety of artists,
Rafael, inspired by pictures of Paul Klee, is following as a first child.
After a visit to the museum of art
where we were looking at the picture *Black Spot* by Wassily Kandinsky,
Latifa, Jathursa, Alissa, and Leyla begin to follow Ismail's example.
Other children are following Latifa's tree with red apples.
Now we have a lot of pictures of apple trees;
and compositions with beautiful colors are painted.
Soon, a big heart in expressive colors
becomes a favorite object to be painted too.

Trying, copying, risking, composing.
I think that Ismail has prepared the way for other children
And for many pictures which are created now.
Ismail was giving others the inducement to go back and find their roots
by painting colored stripes, spots, and points.
Ismail's joy and interest in colors is still extending.
I'm never forcing him to paint an object.

And what happened with his figurative development?
I can simply tell: I am very surprised and impressed
by the expressive sketch of his mask.

K: It seems to me that this example doesn't represent a specific intermodal process as the mask process or the process with opposites. What are you wanting to show in this example?

E: That's right. Here I would like to show other effects of intermodal working. I was really touched by the way Ismail progressed during his time in my class. Through watercolors Ismail could get in contact with his creative roots very quickly. This example shows very well the importance of the care of the soul. Imagine, being in a foreign country where you cannot understand one word, you cannot decipher the letters, everything is new to you. You are having a serious identity crisis. At that moment, teachers allow you to create whatever you like. Anything is good, as long as no harm is done to

**Photograph 8:** Ismail's Sketch of His Mask

others. You have time to play, to create, and to think. At the same time, you can observe what's going on in the room. I know you would like that kind of space.

K: Were you ever afraid that a child like Ismail wouldn't learn mathematics or reading? Ismail had already lost much time for learning. He entered school when he was nine years old. Now you are using valuable time for painting instead of learning mathematics or reading and writing.

E: I don't think that way. There is no lost time. Because of moving to our country, because of being unschooled for nine years, Ismail went through a crisis. I think painting opened Ismail and enabled him to overcome his fear. Ismail and I developed a good relationship. He urgently needed response, and he started to like coming to school. That's the basis for learning. Within a good atmosphere where basic needs are fulfilled, everyone can learn in a better way. That's my opinion, and one that is supported by Maslow's hierarchy of needs. On the other hand, we started learning mathematics, reading, and writing on the first day of school, slowly and without pressure. During the time in my class, Ismail became a strong member of the class; he learned to read, to write, and to calculate. And he likes these cognitive skills too. He now attends a regular class; however, his cognitive skills are still quite weak in comparison to the others. But his personal progress is average, and his personality has grown.

K: You mentioned that Ismail got to be a strong member of the group. You describe in the portrait of Ismail his influence, his inducement on others. You describe that others got inspired by him, Latifa, and others. This seems to be important in your work.

E: It's important for the development of social competence, ego strength, and identity. The students also have other experiences which enrich and widen identity and knowledge. Social education happens through encounter, sharing, and mutual inspiration. I really had the impression that the class was developing as a whole.

K: You brought the children in contact with works of famous artists. What role do these kinds of encounters play in your work?

E: I would love to do it more, but even once is better then never. One reason is to show the students that they are not doing *childish* things. They need to see that their work is embedded in a common cultural context. It should increase the value of their work. I encourage them because they are just beginning to see themselves in new ways.

K: You describe the reaction of Ismail and others very positively.

E: I think, most of the children got inspired. They really liked seeing that famous artists were doing *the same things* they were doing. As I mentioned, Rafael got inspired by the colors by Paul Klee. Jananij, a Tamil girl, got inspired by a pigeon of Pablo Picasso. She was fascinated that the pigeon was drawn by only five lines. She copied it many times. In comparison to Picasso's pigeon, her pigeons got to be very dynamic birds. Since then, such a bird appears in nearly every picture. To conclude, I would like to tell a little story about what happened in the museum of art: Before going to the museum, we played music to painted pictures. We painted pictures to our taped music. In the museum, the museum teacher brought us to the picture *Black Spot* by Wassily Kandinsky. There, the teacher asked the children, what they thought. Sarujan shouted: "That's music!" The museum teacher looked very puzzled. She never expected such an answer. But she agreed with this possibility. Too bad we didn't bring our instruments with us. This work of Kandinsky could really be a good score. I would like to play to it myself.

## Fulfillment of Needs

The satisfaction of elementary needs is a precondition for successful learning. Maslow differentiates within the hierarchy of needs six groups of needs. Nodari (1989) illustrates these groups as follows:

Nodari (1989) mentions important facts which have to be taken into consideration: The more the basic needs (primary physical needs, needs

**Figure 2:** Hierarchy of Needs According to Maslow (Nodari 1989, p. 40)

for safety, needs for belongingness and love, needs for esteem) are fulfilled, the more these needs will decline. On the other hand, the more the intellectual needs and the needs for self-actualization are fulfilled, the more these needs increase. Needs on the higher level only develop if the basic needs are satisfied. Nodari writes: "For a successful acquisition of the German language the following preconditions have to be fulfilled: The children have to feel comfortable and secure in their surroundings. They have to be accepted and esteemed as integral members of the class" (p. 40). The portrayal of Ismail represents the importance of the fulfillment of the basic needs so that the intellectual needs and the needs for self-actualization may develop.

## Development of Language–A Summary

To summarize these three examples of practical work at school, I would like to again emphasize the dialogues that are so important for linguistic development and for second language acquisition: To be in dialogue with oneself, with others, with the written language, and with the formal language.

### To Be in Dialogue with Oneself

When playing and painting, when searching for and finding solutions, thoughts are flowing, questions arise, old and new songs are hummed or sung—alone, in contact with an inner voice, preoccupied with oneself. One important goal: Their own inner stories and dialogues should be kept vivid. As a matter of distress from not knowing the common spoken language, a child shouldn't also fall inwardly silent: Where there is expression, there is also hope. On two different occasions, I asked seven students about their inner thinking. I interviewed each child individually.

The first interviews took place during a lesson when the children were coloring mandalas. I asked the following questions of seven students:

- "Do you think when coloring?" Five children answered "yes." One child answered "no," one child "sometimes."
- "Do you think in your mother tongue or in German?" One child mentioned German, four children mentioned that they would think in both languages, and one child didn't know.
- "What did you think?" All six children could give an answer: "I like it." "When I'm grown up, I will paint beautifully." "I thought about colors." "I thought that my mandala would turn like a spiral." "I thought that it will be beautiful." "In handicraft, I did something similar."

The second interview took place after the mask performance. I asked three questions of seven students:

- "Did you think during the mask performance?" All of the children answered "yes."
- "Did you think in your mother tongue or in German?" Three children mentioned their mother tongues, two mentioned German, and one mentioned that she thought in both languages. One boy answered: "I thought in a language, which doesn't exist. I mean, it exists within me."
- "What did you think?" Three children didn't remember what they had thought. The other answers were: "I said to myself: Play and play and play . . ." "Do I need another shirt?—And: I have to play well." "I thought that I would fail and everyone would laugh. And further: "I don't have to be afraid, I won't die." "I thought that my somersault was great." And: "I like to play."

The students use language when acting or drawing. And which language they use is not yet decisive. Important are direct and primary experiences, through which important development of language as well as development in other fields take place.

## To Be in Dialogue with Others

Language happens in many uncountable dialogues and conversations during work, during breaks from work, when asking for help or for feedback, when receiving instructions, etc. New vocabulary is gained when applying new material, new tools, and when discussing work. Here, language happens and is exercised in a very authentic, embedded context.

## To Be in Dialogue with the Written Language

During the process, Ismail wrote a short story to his picture *Beautiful Colors*. First he wrote a draft. I rewrote this draft in correct German sentences. Then, Ismail copied these sentences in his best handwriting on a colored sheet. He glued his story on the picture. At home, he learned to read his sentences. The next day, he presented his picture and his story to the whole class. In addition, he read all the stories of the other students. This is only one example of how written language can be included and learned. There are further opportunities such as writing school diaries or working journals, or reading texts and stories of former students, etc.

## To Be in Dialogue with the Formal Language

All the many dialogues which take place during an intermodal process allow us to identify specific deficiencies of a student or of a whole group of students. According to the actual situation and goals, and according to the level and needs of the student(s), significant deficiencies may be transferred into formal training. This may be a grammatical subject, spelling exercises, lessons in reading, work on the structure of a text, etc. In any case, the units of formal training should support a better linguistic understanding and should help to widen and to deepen the language performance of the student(s).

# Chapter 4

# Theoretical Frames

## An Art Orientated Approach

Art is important in itself and, therefore, should have its place in education. In personal artistic expression a human being comes again and again to his or her limits of knowledge, skill, and ability. To progress in these areas, it's a basic need to be guided with patience, to work under direction, and to practice. Contrasting these tasks, the intermodal method calls for other artistic aspects to be developed.

When applying art in the method of intermodal learning, keep in mind that the goal is not to practice special artistic skills. Knill (1979) refers to Piaget and emphasizes that organic patterns always develop from a diffuse to a more differentiated state. The development is based on the principle of accommodation and assimilation. The process of interchange between accommodation and assimilation enables optimal learning. Knill argues that this is true as well for the development of feelings and sensations.

According to Knill (1979) the first and basic goal is the development of sensitivity, i.e., the development of the competencies of awareness and expression. Children have to develop their sensitivity toward subtly differentiated listening, seeing, touching, and moving. They have to gain sensitivity for the specific qualities and characteristics of different materials. Every experience, every exploration with a certain material leads to a more subtle differentiation. Knill builds four categories of differentiation in awareness and expression. The four categories (according Knill, 1979, p. 52) are:

- I A: The classes of the source material (e.g., wool or sound of the human voice).

- I B: The qualities of the source material (e.g., thick, twisted, red, loud, penetrating, short).
- II A: Characteristics of the structure (e.g., closely woven or a fast rhythm).
- II B: Form/shape of the structure (e.g., symmetrical, tight fitting, sequential).

Knill (1979) emphasizes that artistic work within I A (classes of source material) and I B (quality) don't need any special manual skills, but that it does enable the development of competence in expression. He found that the ability to differentiate within I A and I B is a precondition to differentiate within II A and II B. To get in contact with the content and the meaning of an artistic work, experiences and explorations in all the four parts are absolutely necessary.

I would like to focus on categories I A and I B for music, visual art, and movement, because these categories build the basis for further learning. Therefore, they are much more important for the described work within a multicultural context than are categories II A and II B. As I discussed earlier, to continue to explore in basic areas helps children to find their inner roots and connect their former home with their new home. Exploring within these basic categories corresponds to the natural developmental process and helps children to develop their abilities of awareness and differentiation which leads to cognitive understanding.

*1. Music: Communication through sound* (according to Knill 1979, pp. 55–56): The material through which music is expressed consists of sound and silence. The material can be differentiated by the classes or qualities of a sound.

- I A: Classes of sound material: sound, tone, noise, mixtures, etc.
- I B: Qualities of sound material: volume (loud, soft), tone color (bright, sinister, metallic, muffled, etc.), pitch (high, low), time (period of the sounds, intervals between sounds), space (where the sound is coming from).

*2. Visual art: Communication through pictures* (according to Knill 1979, pp. 62–63): The material through which visual art is expressed is differentiated according to its classes and qualities.

- I A: Classes of material: wood, stone, paper, plastic, metal, clay, wire, plants, animals, water, fire, colors, pencil, ink, etc.

- I B: Qualities of material: color, weight, texture, form, contour, size, etc.

*3. Dance: Communication through movement* (according to Knill 1979, pp. 68–70): The following shows how to differentiate structures of movements which correspond with sensorimotor intelligence.

- Sources of movements: parts of the body (hands, feet, head, shoulder, etc.), kind of movement (going, jumping, breathing, etc.), equipment (ball, string, towels, etc.)
- Quality of the movement: effort (free, restricted, easily, strong, suddenly, direct, indirect, etc.), shape (body orientated figure, surrounding orientated figure, process orientated figure, etc.)

Through my practical work with children I have learned that often the best advice to give children was: "Play, just play with colors, with clay, with instruments, with the meaning of turning around when moving, when going on stage, etc." In doing this, I too started to play. I was a model for the children. I didn't play in a childish way. I played in my very own way with clay, with colors, with movements, etc. One possibility for gaining a deeper exploring effect is a restriction; such as giving the children only two colors plus white or black for painting. Soon, the children will start to mix and find lots of colors which are different, but very close to each other. They start to talk about making certain colors. As time passes, the classroom becomes a color lab. When communicating through music, special attention has to be put on the selection of the instruments. Appropriate instruments to fulfill the demands of I A and I B are all rhythmical instruments, and all melodical instruments with fixed sequences of sounds, e.g., piano, psaltery, xylophone, harmonica, etc. Less appropriate are instruments with unfixed sequences of sounds like all strings or wind instruments. These instruments demand advanced technical skills and easily frustrate children.

For immigrant children, art can be a common language providing emotional literacy; it will enable them to open up. Through art, they can learn. Many goals can be reached through working with art. Art in education can be:

- for itself, for creativity
- for expression of emotions and feelings
- for regeneration and comfort
- for self-confidence and self-esteem

- for socialization, sharing, communication
- for building bridges between cultures
- for learning, exploring, and experiencing of the basic skills in art
- for learning a dominant language
- for learning school context
- for developing of awareness, expression, and sensitivity

This list is by no means a complete one. Working with art always means working toward several goals, except perhaps when *art for itself* is the central goal. But even in that case, goals like regeneration, comfort at school, self-confidence and self-esteem, developing of awareness, expression and sensitivity, etc., are probably touched. I have come to the conclusion that when working with the intermodal method, a child is educated in a very integral manner. I have found that besides goals which I'm able to measure quite well (e.g., learning a dominant language, learning school context, learning basic skills in art) less measurable goals will be reached, goals which belong mostly to the common underlying proficiency (see p. 61 & 63) or to higher interpersonal and intrapersonal competencies (see chapter 4).

When starting intermodal work with a class that is unfamiliar with the method, I recommend starting slowly. The children have to first become familiar with the method before they will feel secure. Repetition in varied forms helps to establish the method (see p. 21). Further, it's important to present frames and rules very clearly in order to guarantee children the support they need so they can focus on the activity (see p. 21). Often, the products of the children don't fit into common aesthetic standards. Therefore, teachers may need to set these standards aside and look at the children's work according to the goals of the intermodal method.

## Levels of Language Proficiency

As we have seen, intermodal learning is not only a method for working on the surface level of second language acquisition. Intermodal learning is a very holistic method that helps to develop many different aspects of the individual. Therefore, intermodal learning helps to develop deeper levels of language proficiency.

The metaphor of the *dual iceberg*, which was introduced by Cummins (1984), represents the level of effect of the intermodal method—the deeper and therefore less visible and less easily measurable level of knowledge, ability, and skills. Cummins's arguments are based on much research by him and other researchers in Canada, the United States, South Africa, and Europe. Cummins (1984) writes: "A considerably longer period of time is required [for non-native English speakers] to learn sufficient English to perform at the same level in academic tasks as native English speakers than is usually required to converse fluently in face-to-face situations" (p. 136). Why are these students not able to achieve the same academic performance?

Cummins (1984) refers to Shuy, who introduced the iceberg metaphor to point out the distinction between the visible and therefore quantifiable, formal aspects of language (e.g., pronunciation, basic vocabulary, grammar) and the less visible and therefore less easily measured aspects of language (e.g., semantic and functional meaning). The first is defined as "the manifestation of language proficiency in everyday communicative contexts" (everyday communicative skills), the second may be understood as "the manipulation of language in decontextualized academic situations" (p. 137).

Cummins (1984) emphasizes that most language teachers, whether they teach the first language or a second language, try to develop language proficiency, functional as well as communicative skills, by concentrating on the surface forms. Thus, they neglect the fact that language acquisition is developing from the deeper communicative functions of language to the surface forms.

The distinction of basic interpersonal communication skills (conversational proficiency) and cognitive/academic language proficiency is ex-

**Figure 3:** Surface and Deeper Levels of Language Proficiency (Cummins, 1984, p. 138)

pressed in iceberg metaphor. Referring to the iceberg, Cummins (1984) argues: "The major points embodied in BICS/CALP [basic interpersonal communicative skill; the cognitive/academic language proficiency] distinction are that some heretofore neglected aspects of language proficiency are considerably more relevant for students' cognitive and academic progress than are the surface manifestations of proficiency frequently focused on by educators, and the educators' failure to appreciate these differences can have particularly unfortunate consequences for minority students," i.e., non-native English speakers (pp. 137–138).

As seen, non-native-English-speaking students normally have much higher communicative language skills than cognitive/academic language skills. They gain their communicative skills more or less within an embedded context, mostly within the everyday world outside the classroom. On the other hand, many of the linguistic and academic demands of the classroom happen within a limited context. Cummins (1984) refers to research from Donaldson (1978) that elucidates aspects of the relationships between language proficiency and academic development. She points out that ". . . young children's early thought processes and use of language develop within a 'flow meaningful context' in which the logic of words is subjugated to perception of the speaker's intentions and salient features of the situation. Thus, children's (and adults') normal productive speech is embedded within a context of fairly immediate goals, intentions, and familiar patterns of events. However, thinking and language that move behind the bounds of meaningful interpersonal context make entirely different demands on the individual" (p. 140). There are conclusive indications that children are able to achieve much higher cognitive performance when the subject is presented and taught in an embedded context, or within one which is personally meaningful. It is a fact that an unnecessary disembedding of academic tasks from students' out-of-school experiences, specifically during the first years of school and actually regardless of the age of the students, contributes significantly to educational difficulties. Further, Cummins (1984) writes about the meaning for immigrant students. He concludes: "The more context-embedded the initial L 2 [second language] input, the more comprehensible it is likely to be, and paradoxically, the more successful in ultimately developing L 2 skills in context-reduced situations. A central reason why minority students have often failed to develop high levels of L 2 academic skills is because their initial instruction has emphasized context-reduced communication insofar as instruction has been through English and unrelated to their prior out-of-school experience" (p. 141).

Cummins (1984) describes the first (L1) and second language (L 2) academic skills as being interdependent. He depicts this as the *common underlying proficiency* by referring to the iceberg metaphor, which he turns into a *dual iceberg* to represent the bilingual proficiency. It is "a 'dual-iceberg' in which common cross-lingual proficiencies underlie the obviously different surface manifestations of each language. The interdependence of common underlying proficiency principle implies that experience with *either* language can promote development of the proficiency underlying both languages, given adequate motivation and exposure to both either in school or in the wider environment" (p. 143).

The following examples will further illustrate the meaning of the *dual iceberg*: If a child has learned to read in the Greek alphabet, he or she has only to learn the Latin letters and their specific pronunciations in English or German in order to apply the same skill to the new language. For a Tamil child who is literate in the Tamil syllabary, the common ground is much smaller, but it still exists. The child has achieved the ability to transfer words and sentences into symbols, and to decipher these symbols with words and sentences. Therefore, there is a significant difference between such a child and a totally illiterate one. If a child has learned in one language, e.g., to examine a plant and to transfer the examined facts into oral and written language; if a child has learned to write a text; if a child has learned to interpret a written mathematical problem and to convert it into calculations; if a child has learned to differentiate and to find correlations, etc., he or she is theoretically able to apply all these abilities in any

**Figure 4:** The '*dual iceberg*' Representation of Bilingual Proficiency (Cummins, 1984, p. 143)

other language. The ability to perform an academic task is not dependent on linguistic ability concerning grammar or vocabulary in one or another language. Of course a good knowledge of grammar and a wide vocabulary makes the work much easier. To be successful in academic tasks requires the abilities to analyze, to synthesize, to evaluate, and to develop concepts and strategies to convert and to act.

Cummins (1984) argues for bilingual educational programs. They have found that such schools aren't intended to be an advantage only for bright children. Cummins cites Malherbe (1969, within Cummins 1984): "Not only do they more than hold their own in their first language (in comparison to equivalent IQ children in monolingual schools), but in their second language their gain was nearly twice as big as that registered by the higher intelligence groups" (p. 146). This important demand is hardly fulfilled within the context of our school in Zurich where children are speaking more than forty different languages. Therefore it's not possible to teach them bilingually. But we can use and apply *common underlying languages*—the artistic languages. A student once referred to body language as the *language of our world.*

Another demand of Cummins is to support academic skills within an embedded context. This means that teachers have to focus on the underlying proficiencies as well. As far as the direction of language acquisition develops from deeper communicative functions to the surface forms, the deeper functions build the basis for all languages a person is going to learn. Teachers can and need to build on the interdependence of L 1 and L 2. They should teach and support the students in the common underlying realm.

The method of intermodal learning, as shown in the three examples, is a method which supports that demand. It works intently in the common underlying realm; it is a context embedded method. As we have seen, the children didn't learn just the German language, they learned much more.

## The Theory of Multiple Intelligences

The theory of multiple intelligences was introduced by Howard Gardner in the early eighties. Gardner (1993a) extends and reformulates our customary view regarding the meaning of the terms *intellect* and *intelligence.*

According to a large group of sources on studies of prodigies, gifted individuals, brain-damaged patients, *idiots savants*, normal children, normal adults, experts in different lines of work, and individuals from diverse cultures, and according to eight specific criteria of an intelligence, Gardner

(1993a) defines seven different intelligences: *Linguistic Intelligence*; *Musical Intelligence*; *Logical-Mathematical Intelligence*; *Spatial Intelligence*; *Bodily-Kinesthetic Intelligence*; *Interpersonal Intelligence*; and *Intrapersonal Intelligence*. Gardner (1993a) doesn't pretend this list to be a complete one. In a lecture given in October 1996 in St. Gallen, Switzerland, he introduced two new areas he was researching on at that time: A *Naturalist Intelligence* which focuses abilities according to nature; and a *Spiritual* or *Existential Intelligence* which focuses abilities on the fundamental questions surrounding our existence and existence of truth in myth, art, religion, psychology, and science. Gardner has since proclaimed proof of the *naturalist intelligence*.

Gardner (1993a) doesn't differentiate between intelligence and talent, but he distinguishes among intelligences, domains, and fields. He writes, "At the level of the individual, it is proper to speak about one or more human *intelligences*, or human intellectual proclivities, that are part of our birthright. These intelligences may be thought of in neurobiological

**Table 3:** The Multiple Intelligences I (Based on Huser, 1999)

| | |
|---|---|
| Linguistic Intelligence | The ability to use language aptly to express and to reflect one's own thoughts; the ability to understand others. |
| Musical Intelligence | The ability to think in musical patterns; the ability to perceive, recognize, rearrange, and to perform rhythms and patterns. |
| Logical-Mathematical Intelligence | The ability to deal with calculations, numbers, and quantities. |
| Spatial Intelligence | The ability to recognize visual things in a correct way and to experiment with it in one's mind; the ability to imagine the world spatially. |
| Bodily-Kinesthetic Intelligence | The ability to use the whole body or parts of the body agilely and fluidly. |
| Intrapersonal Intelligence | The ability to control impulses; to know personal limits; to deal with one's own emotions in a constructive way; to be aware of one's own inner connections and relations. |
| Interpersonal Intelligence | The ability to understand others and to communicate in an empathic manner with them; the ability to guide people. |
| Naturalist Intelligence | The ability to observe, to differentiate, and to recognize living things; to develop a sensitivity for phenomenon of nature. |
| Existential Intelligence | The ability to recognize the significant questions of our existence and to formulate answers. (Not definitely proven at this time.) |

terms. Human beings are born into cultures that house a large number of *domains*—disciplines, crafts, and other pursuits in which one can become enculturated and then be assessed in terms of the level of competence one has attained. While domains, of course, involve human beings, they can be thought of in an impersonal way" (p. xvi).

A domain refers to a cultural activity, such as a lawyer, a teacher, etc. Nearly every domain requires proficiency in a set of different intelligences. For example, a dancer requires intelligences beyond the bodily-kinesthetic intelligence, e.g., musical intelligence and the personal intelligences. On the other hand, a piano player needs to mobilize the bodily-kinesthetic intelligence as well. A surgeon has to have not only an extraordinary spatial intelligence but also a high bodily-kinesthetic intelligence regarding the sensitive motor activity. Gardner (1993a) writes, "During socialization, intercourse occurs principally between the individual and the domains of the cultures" (p. xvii). Gardner (1993a) defines the *field* as "a sociological construct—(which) includes the people, institutions, award mechanism, and so forth that render judgments about qualities of individual performance" (p. xvii).

The following three arguments should prevent misunderstanding of the theory of multiple intelligences. In the lecture given in 1996 (see above), Gardner stressed that an intelligence is not the same as a learning or working style. Second, Gardner (1993a) emphasizes that an intelligence is not equivalent to a sensory system because in no case has a sensory system turned out to involve only a single intelligence. Third, in ordinary life the different intelligences may not be recognized autonomously, because they are working in harmony.

I will now focus again on the seven intelligences. Gardner (1993b; and lecture, see above) illustrates each intelligence with a specific domain or activity of mastery and an outstanding personality who initiated an evolutionary process in his or her discipline in the twentieth century. Even though these personalities are protagonists of one of the seven intelligences, they all had the whole range of human competencies at their disposal.

Regarding the theme of this book, I will focus on the linguistic intelligence. Core operations of languages are, according to Gardner (1993a), sensitivity to the meaning of words, sensitivity to the order of words, sensitivity to the sounds, rhythms, inflections, and meters of words, and sensitivity to the different functions of language. Everyone possesses these abilities to a certain degree, but the poet is a very gifted person in this realm. Therefore, I have drawn the conclusion that one task of education should be to promote sensitivity to support linguistic competence. Gardner (1993a) identifies linguistic intelligence as the intellectual competence

**Table 4:** The Multiple Intelligences II (Based on Gardner 1993b)

| Intelligence | Domain or activity of mastery; professions | Personality of the 20th century |
|---|---|---|
| Linguistic Intelligence | Poet; Writer; Author; Story Teller; Master of Rhetoric | T. S. Eliot (1888–1965) Poet |
| Musical Intelligence | Conductor; Composer | Igor Stravinsky (1882–1971) Composer |
| Logical-Mathematical Intelligence | Scientist | Albert Einstein (1879–1955) Professor for Theoretical Physics |
| Spatial Intelligence | Chess; Visual Artist; Surgeon | Pablo Picasso (1881–1973) Visual Artist |
| Bodily-Kinesthetic Intelligence | Dancer; Athlete; Actor | Martha Graham (1894–1991) Dancer |
| Interpersonal Intelligence | Leader in Politics, Religion, Trade, Health Service; Teacher | Mahatma Gandhi (1869–1948) Political and Spiritual Leader |
| Intrapersonal Intelligence | Psychologist; Psychotherapist; Scientist in Psychology and Therapy | Sigmund Freud (1856–1939) Neurologist and Psychologist |

". . . that seems most widely and most democratically shared across human species" (p. 78). Beside these core operations Gardner (1993a) names four further linguistic aspects: The rhetorical aspect and the mnemonic potential of language, its role in explanation, and its potential to explain its own activities (metalinguistic analysis). The interest in this last ability is mainly restricted to Western or other scientifically orientated cultures.

In most situations language is used as a tool. The emphasis is not on the language itself but on the message, the transferred ideas. The perfect choice of words is not as important as in a literary work. Gardner (1993a) argues that oral and written forms of language are based for the most part on the same capacities. But to express oneself in writing, additional skills are needed because of the absence of nonlinguistic sources like gestures, voice, surrounding situations, etc. Gardner (1993a) emphasizes the importance of the written word in our culture. We gain a lot of information by reading, and thus the perfect written expression plays an important role. Traditional cultures cultivate and emphasize the oral language, where rhetorical performances and word play are important.

The existence of many different ways of acquiring and representing knowledge is a well-known fact. An example is "the literate person who can read the instructions perfectly but cannot assemble the machine, and the illiterate person who can determine at a glance just where every part fits" (Gardner 1991, p. 14). Gardner (1991) distinguishes three different characteristics of the learner, the intuitive (also natural, naive, universal) learner with an intuitive understanding; the scholastic (also traditional student) learner with a rote, ritualized, and conventional understanding; and the disciplinary expert (also skilled person) with a disciplinary and genuine understanding. Disciplinary students are able to successfully transfer their knowledge to new settings. Regarding genuine understanding, Gardner (1991) writes, "An important symptom of an emerging understanding is the capacity to represent a problem in a number of different ways and to approach its solution from varied vantage points; a single, rigid representation is unlikely suffice" (p. 18). Therefore, a second task of schools should be the support of gaining this ability.

Gardner (1991) criticizes our schools as "heavily biased toward linguistic modes of instruction and assessment and, to a somewhat lesser degree, toward logical-quantitative modes as well" (p. 12). In his lecture (see above) Gardner described the typical professional working field of a person with highly developed linguistic and logical-mathematical intelligences: "A bureaucrat to be sent to a colony." Further, he emphasized the increasing importance of the personal intelligences in our rapidly changing world, especially for people in leading positions. The development of the personal intelligences may help in bearing crisis, in finding one's way, and in taking up one's place within a new community. I would add that people with well-developed personal intelligences can help solve problems within a multicultural, democratic society.

## The Intermodal Method and the Method of Working with Core Ideas

The method of *Working with Core Ideas* is an interactive and interdisciplinary didactic, also called *Learning in One's Own Way*. A comparison of that method with the intermodal method shows that the methods are related to each other. Central for both methods is individual participation and dialogue within the learning group and with other people who are interested in the same subject.

Ruf and Gallin (1996) argue that subject-specific terminology should never serve as the main goal but as method for scientific work. Emphasis should be placed on a personal examination of the subject and its problems and on discourse with other people who are working on the same material. They point out that learners who are not yet capable of using the right terminology should first use their familiar colloquial language. Step by step, the learners will become familiar with terminology through personal definition and through divergent dialogues. Working with core ideas allows the learner to move between the familiar colloquial language and the subjectspecific terminology. Ruf and Gallin propose this type of learning experience for math and language classes.

### The Three Phases of Learning

The method of working with core ideas differentiates between three phases (Berger-Kündig, 1996; translation by the author):

1. The singular phase/level:
   - Relation between the subject and the individual, one's own world. (Authentic encounter, associative approach.)
   - Individuality is the basis for further steps.
   - The personal world is the starting point for the lessons.

2. The divergent phase:
   - Exchange between learners (oral and written).
   - Dialogue between students.

3. The regular phase/level:
   - Approach to the subject.
   - Approach to the field.
   - Approach to science.
   - Adoption of rules.
   - Adoption of procedures.
   - Orientation on standards.

An important aspect of working with core ideas is the accompanying working journal. Its purposes are: Documentation of the individual process and review and comparison of the experience with other students and the teacher.

The singular (or personal) phase is an associative phase, an authentic approach, within which the students should describe the effect of the subject on themselves. The goal of this phase is to overcome fear of the subject and to develop curiosity. First one's own personal position should be found. This phase should mobilize all the psychological resources available. The important point here is what happens between the subject and the student. The teacher's role is to listen, to support the student in getting in touch with the subject.

For a better understanding, Ruf and Gallin (1996) introduce the following analogy: Every kind of art asks for an authentic personal definition, because every work is unique and asks for a personal response. Quality works of art have the very special power to ask again and again for personal reactions, as if someone is experiencing a well known work for the first time. The confrontation with art should be a model for education. It is important to arouse sensibility and to provide suitable tools for authentic encounter. Ruf and Gallin (1996) state that the main medium for this is language.

## The Meaning for the Intermodal Method

The singular, associative phase, the authentic encounter, can also be fulfilled by using different kinds of art, as I have done with my students during intermodal lessons: To find a personal idea, a personal position by drawing a picture of one's own needs; to have dialogue with the others by presenting the pictures; to crystallize by writing a story to the picture; to respond by playing music to a chosen object on the picture; to respond again by drawing the music of each of the children. Such a process helps students to get in deeper contact with their own work, to listen to foreign works, and to give feedback. Art is a different tool than language for getting in contact, to find one's own position, to gain sensibility, to get in dialogue. It leads and opens to the regular world: In my class this led to the story *Peter and the Wolf* by Serge Prokofiew and later to an impressive encounter with two pictures in the Museum of Art—a medieval picture of the Archangel Michael, and the picture *Schwarzer Fleck* [black spot] by Wassily Kandinsky (see p. 50).

During the lessons, we moved between the singular and the divergent phases. The divergent phase means to get into dialogue, to present products and get responses and feedback. The child must present his/her work in a way that it can be understood by others. During the lessons I realized that the children became more and more explicit. They acted for themselves, but they also started to think and to act for the group. They approached the work of Prokofiew, and they tried to interpret and understand his musical story. They got into dialogue with the medieval St. Michael and with the work of Kandinsky. They got inspiration from them and from other pictures on postcards (Klee, Picasso, Monet, Chagall, etc.). I can see elements of these encounters with the regular world in the students pictures.

In my class the working journal was replaced by an album of artwork. We collected the pictures and put them together in a continuing form in an album. I gave the children a chance to listen to the music again. I reviewed the work by remembering the steps we went through during the whole process. A good medium for this work is narration by the teacher. To review means to fulfill the process and to preview for what will come next.

During the quasi nonverbal phase of the child, when the verbal expression in the second language is very limited, art offers as an important opportunity to learn important steps for working with core ideas. Further, I'm certain that the inclusion of the artistic *languages* in the method of working with core ideas will be a valuable addition. Art is central to gaining sensibility and awareness. Art opens the person, mobilizes psychological resources, expands consciousness, and leads to a new reality. Through this process which includes lots of self experience, lots of exploration in the new world, children learn language which is connected with the new context. Personal development, cognitive as well as emotional, and learning a new language go hand in hand.

### Concluding Comparison

In both methods, working with core ideas and working with the intermodal method, moving between singular and divergent phases, between individual and social phases are important for presenting, sharing, feedback, and appreciation. It is a dialogical process. Essential for both methods is to find common languages, general terminology as well as symbolic terminology. Important in both methods is the carrying out of all steps and phases during the whole process. The process itself as well as the works are central. Both methods have central characteristics in common and, therefore, they have an inspiring and stimulating effect on each other.

## The Underlying Concept of Development

**Development**

is a process<br>
of movement and balance<br>
of balance and movement<br>
of movement and balance<br>
–life long<br>
or even longer

Today, human development is understood as a life-spanning process which runs in accordance with certain laws. It starts at the very beginning of one's life and ends with the last breath. Each step an individual has fulfilled is an irreversible one. Baacke (1991, within Gudjons 1995) defines the term of development as the following: "Development means the integral change of a person which often is crucially conditioned by the organic substratum, but which includes cognitive, affective, and other facts" (p. 117; translation by the author). The human being is seen as an interactive creature who is constructing a meaningful world for him- or herself.

## The Theory of Equilibration by Piaget

Equilibration means finding balance in one's life, which is an interactive process between a developing individual and the changing world, between subject and object, between assimilation and accommodation. Kegan (1996) describes equilibration as "a process of adaptation shaped by the tension between the assimilation of new experience to the old *grammar* and the accommodation of the old grammar to new experience. This eternal conversation is panorganic" (pp. 43–44). Further he writes "that this conversation is not one of continuous augmentation, but is marked by periods of dynamic stability or balance followed by periods of instability and qualitatively new balance" (p. 44).

Such a process is always a process of differentiation. It encompasses what Piaget calls *decentration*. Decentration means to lose the old center; therefore it means entering a state of crisis. "Central to the experience of qualitative change or decentration (. . .) are the affects of loss—anxiety and depression" (p. 82). But such a crisis means the beginning of a new stage of life as well. A person is now able to see with new eyes. She (or he) learns to see the former situation from a detached position because she is no longer embedded in the old situation. She can see the distinction between herself and the world in a more differentiated way. But again, she is now embedded in a qualitative new subjective world. Kegan (1996) calls it *recentration*, the recovery of a new center. Now she will live in that stage of life until the next decentration enters her life. The underlying rhythm of personal development presents itself as "*object creating* must mean *subject losing*," but "*subject losing* can lead to *object finding*" (p. 83). Kegan (1996) argues, "This evolutionary motion is the prior (or grounding) phenomenon in personality; this process or activity, this adaptive conversation, is the very source of, and the unifying context for, thought and feeling" (p. 44). Freud researched affective development, and Piaget researched cognitive development. Seen from the neo-Piagetian perspective these two phenomena are only two dimensions of one basic process—the evolutionary activity of decentration and recentration. It's "an activity of equilibration, of preserving or renegotiating the balance between what is taken as subject or self and what is taken as object or other" (Kegan 1996, p. 81). Further, Kegan summarizes, "In this sense, evolutionary activity is intrinsically cognitive, but is no less affective; we *are* this activity and we experience it" (p. 81). It's the experience of "defending, surrendering, and reconstructing" (p.82); a quite painful process because of the separation from a well-known structure.

What is the motivation for such a painful evolutionary process? On a philosophical and spiritual level, it's the striving of the human being to perfect oneself morally, mentally, and spiritually. On another level, according to neo-Piagetians, it's the striving for a balanced state which seems to be the most comfortable and convenient one within a particular context. An individual tends to equilibrate discrepancy between the subjective and the objective world. One tends to coordinate the inner and outer world, and all inconsistencies by building more and more complex structures. In doing so, the individual doesn't tend toward the old reality, but tries to find a meaning for the present situation and searches to understand the new and even more complex situation.

## The Model of Development by Erikson

According to Erikson, an individual gains identity through coping with eight different crises which are interdependent and subject to fundamental laws. Erikson (1994) calls this organismic principle epigenesis. In Erikson's terms, crisis is a constitutive and integral part of normal development. Every stage of development has its special psychosocial crisis with its special main theme. It's a question of solving the crisis by struggling and balancing between two orientations, the positive and the negative aspects of every theme, e.g., basic trust vs. basic mistrust, autonomy vs. shame and doubt, initiative vs. guilt, etc. The individual will leave the stage in a certain balanced condition somewhere between the two tendencies. The quality of that condition is important for all further stages.

I think that we carry all the stages within us as potential. We do not lose the potential of one stage when we reach another one. As we gain new insight and knowledge which changes our point of view and consciousness, we can go back and forth between levels depending on the context of our immediate situation. This can happen unconsciously and/or unintentionally, e.g., by regression, or intentionally by decision to call to mind or to repeat up certain experiences and/or learning steps to get in touch with a specific potential. We can progress or we can remain at very primitive levels all our lives. To some extent, human beings have influence on remaining or proceeding. Educators—parents, teachers, etc.—can support, neglect, or try to avoid development; individuals can try to be open or can try to resist development.

## The Helix as a Symbol of Development

Kegan (1996) describes yearning for belonging and yearning for autonomy to be the two greatest yearnings in human experience. These two great yearnings are in conflict with each other. Kegan describes that conflict as a lifelong tension. He sees every balanced situation as being a temporary solution of a lifelong tension between the yearning for autonomy and belonging. Each balanced state resolves the stress in a different form. During ones life, it's actually a continuous process of back and forth between the two orientations. In one stage the problem is resolved in the favor of autonomy, and in another stage in favor of belonging and conclusion. Actually each gained balance means a certain *im*balanced state because of the lack of the opposite quality. There is always a risk of going to one extreme or the other. Instead of a line, Kegan (1996) chooses a spiral or a helix to depict development. Refusing to define growth only in terms of differentiation and increasing autonomy, he equally places adaptation, i.e., the process of integration, attachment, and inclusion, on the same level. Therefore, he sees the psychological meaning and experience of evolution as a moving and balancing process of differentiation *and* integration.

## Interruptions in the Developmental Process

The existentialist Bollnow (1959) talks about interruptions of the developmental process and the effect on education. As he describes the nature of crisis, he argues that we find crises wherever people have to give up a well loved or well planned way of life. I will now take a closer look at Bollnow's arguments as they relate to children in this type of crisis.

A crisis is a decisive point in what has been a rather steady development of life. It enters like lightning with an unusual intensity, and is often characterized by mortal agony or by an experience of falling into darkness. During a crisis a person loses the sense of time. After the crisis is under control a person often experiences a state of high euphoria with feelings of liberation and happiness. A crisis separates and connects two phases of one's life. It separates and connects two balanced states. Only through coping with a crisis can a human being reach a new quality of life. When talking about moral crisis, Bollnow discusses the time before the crisis occurs. During that phase an individual is slipping slowly and imperceptibly in an irreversible crisis. From my point of view, crises are often foreshadowed, but an individual cannot or perhaps doesn't want to decipher the signs. These can be symptoms of inner restlessness, moodiness, stress, insomnia, lack of appetite, bad dreams, etc. The worst problem is that it cannot be understood unless someone knows about these preceding phases.

What's the meaning of all this for education? Every crisis means endangerment as well as growth and healing. But a crisis is not a subject to be manipulated by educators. The educator's role is to stand by with an empathic attitude without doing anything special. And an educator can try to help to understand the sense of the crisis and to bear with it till the end. Educators need to know about such processes and need to take that knowledge into consideration when reflecting on the educational process. But it shouldn't be the subject of an educational plan.

I want to emphasize the importance of knowing about the preceding phases as well as about the phases of integration. The phases of integration are often forgotten because they are calmer and less obvious than the excited phases of the crisis itself. But these phases are important for a healthy development. School needs to allow space where preparation, regeneration, and integration can happen.

### Interrupted Development of Cognitive Processes

Bollnow (1959) talks about interrupted development in the cognitive field. He says that knowledge itself can be gained through a steady growth process of accumulation. However, this doesn't mean recognition, which is something totally different. Recognition cannot be gained step by step but it enters all at once, like lightning. It's like scales fell from one's eyes, or like an *aha* experience. Bollnow describes the new recognition as a sudden insight, like an inspiration. He emphasizes that one could only prepare with patience for this moment, but has to wait until it enters.

In his book Bollnow (1959) refers to Copei who named that moment *the fruitful moment within the developmental process*. Bollnow describes that moment again as a state of crisis. It occurs with the experience of disruption as well as with the feelings of happiness and liberation. An individual is touched by that moment not only in the intellectual realm but in a very integral way. The preceding phase is often accompanied by a yearning for better and deeper understanding. Such a *fruitful moment* cannot be planned. We have to wait until it happens. It's the power of a fateful element. Such a moment can be the first German word an immigrant child uses on his or her own initiative. After that first step is accomplished, a child will proceed quickly. As seen, an educational process has its limits in being planned. Educators have to find a balance between what can be planned and what is unforeseen. It's a balance between intellect and intuition. And it asks for confidence in the process.

## Awakening within the Educational Development Process

Bollnow (1959) talks about awakening and specifically about its educational aspect. He argues that awakening in an educational context means neither *doing* nor *letting do*, two opposite views in education. The first view has its roots in the Enlightenment, the second view in the philosophy of Rousseau. Bollnow (1959) postulates that only what already exists can be awoken. It means only to get the awakening off the ground with the outer help of an educator. According to Bollnow, it's again an unsteady process, perhaps followed by a phase of being awake and a phase of steady development. Bollnow (1959) refers to Montessori, who uses the term of *awakening*, too. She distinguishes between two different achievements: First, the awakening—the impetus to the child—is the educator's achievement. Second, the educator's achievement ends with that impetus. Further development is only the child's achievement. According to Montessori, an educator's task is to teach others to concentrate, to focus inwardly. She argues that inner composure enables an event which is similar to awakening and which frees mental powers. The consequence is a deep change. It's the awakening of something unexpected.

Seen in this way, growing means something which again and again receives its impetus from the outside but which actually means growth emerging from the inner center. Awakening in education is a repetitive event which enables a certain step of development. This model of awakening has its equivalent in the everyday life of education.

## An Unsteady Helix as Symbol for Development

I like Kegan's (1996) expansion of the line to the helix to symbolize development: It's a symbol which shows the ongoing process of differentiation as well as the necessary achievement of integration. It shows that wintertime, the time for regeneration, belongs to life as well as spring and summertime. The helix symbolizes the resumption of the appearance of the same or similar themes in different qualities during a lifetime. But the helix gives the impression of a steady developmental process. I myself have the image of a spiral which at times is climbing quite steeply, and at other times is merely turning in the same place. It's a spiral full of smooth and rough parts, abrupt steps, and breaks. Further on, the unsteady helix get its impetus from the environment and from interactions with the outside world.

Seen from a symbolic point of view, development means balancing between progression and regression; decentration and recentration; balancing between polarities; balancing between steady and unsteady phases; balancing between doing by giving impetus and letting the child grow from his/her inner impetus; balancing between giving impetus and waiting with patience for the fruitful moment: Moving and balancing, balancing and moving—again and again.

## The Concept of Education

### Education

is a question of an integrative
tightrope walk
between
one side of a coin and the other,
depending on
situation, context, time, and goal.

"Paracelsus, the Master, says:
'Nothing is poisonous.
Everything is poisonous.
It all depends on the dose.'"

(Jürg Federspiel)

When an absolutist system, a monarchy or a dictatorship, is once set, it's meant to be set forever. When a democracy is once introduced, it is subject to be reflected upon, rediscussed, and adapted forever. Democracy is based on the variety and equality within humanity. It is based on dialogues between its members. It is based on a political system which enables the community to process. It is based on self-determining individuals who are concerned about community. Central is neither only the government nor the isolated individual; central is the partnership, the dialogue between the government and the individuals. School has to educate children to be mature members of a democracy. Therefore, education cannot be based on absolute points of view.

During the last decades, our Western world started to learn about Eastern kinds of thinking. We've been inspired by that holistic nonlinear kind of being. Famous contributions to this kind of thinking were made by C. G. Jung in psychology, and H. Hesse in literature, two persons who inspired me as a young adult.

The method of intermodal learning is based on the idea of holistic principles. It claims the existence of different points of view. Nothing can be considered for absolute; nothing can be taken for granted. One side always includes at least part of another side. The focus doesn't lie on one side of the coin but it lies on the area between the two polarities, between the I and Thou, between the I and It. It lies on the dynamic interaction which happens between the two aspects. Central is the dialogical principle which Buber (1983) describes with insistence. In the previous chapter I have touched on examples of the dialogical principle which show the absence of absolute statements like *either this or that*, but the existence of *this and that*, or in the term *as well as*. For example, I described development as movement *and* balance, as differentiation *and* integration; a developmental process as a steady *as well as* an unsteady one; a gained balanced state in the meantime as a kind of imbalanced one; education as doing *as well as* letting grow.

Let's take a closer look at the dialogical principle. Dialogic was introduced by H. L. Goldschmitt in 1944. Herzka (1989) describes dialogic as follows: "Dialogic postulates two thoughts, which none can think simultaneously; or two tendencies, which never can be fulfilled at the same time; or two terms which exclude each other and each indicate an area for itself, but together make up a unit, simultaneously (i.e., not one after the other) and of the same value (i.e., without any claim to superiority or subordination)" (pp. 19–20; translation by the author). A unit as described includes an area which lies between the dual aspects. It's a contradictory area where both sides are involved. This contradiction is not subject to being neutralized. The dynamic and interactive process which takes place in the area between is not to be removed or solved, but to be borne, regulated, and used to benefit. The dialogic principle is based on a relationship which requires continuous acceptance and estimation of different qualities.

The intermodal method follows the dialogical principle. When looking to the past it estimates contributions of divergent philosophies. Each side has its specific qualities, and each quality will once in a while come to the forefront, depending on the situation, the context, the time, and the goal. Applying the dialogical principle in education means oscillating between two dual and therefore excluding qualities. Table 5 shows the main aspects of education and their meanings regarding education as an art and the dialogical principle.

| **One part of the scale considered in the absolute—there is no alternative** | **The tightrope walk of the concept of education as an art** | **The other part of the s considered in the absolu there is no alternati** |
|---|---|---|
| The ideal of Rousseau: . *The naturally good child* Education is damaging. | According to both sides, a child is a natural being but with weak sides which have to be integrated. | The child seen as a *tabula r* Everything has to be insti into a child. |
| Reversible, equal partnerships instead of education. (A. S. Neill: Antiauthoritarian education) Basis: Freedom. | According to both sides, relationship is based on a dialogical attitude and of being critical of authority: It's a specific relationship which exists as a difference between unequal individuals, unequal because of age, role, competence, knowledge . . . , but equal individuals because they are human beings. | Education and relationship a based on difference of comp and power: Authoritarian e with the aspect of obligati |
| Everything is within the child (Rousseau, A .S. Neill): Let the child grow. Don't damage anything. | According to both sides: The *fruitful moment* within the educational process (see p. 75). The individual learner in interaction with the environment. | Everything is outside the ch (Behaviorism): A child nee to be guided, to be advise It needs the intentional inf |
| Strengthening of human beings. Constructing knowledge. | According to both sides, the purpose of education is strengthening of human beings in society and making things clear. | Making things clear. Receiving knowledge. |
| Emancipation from dependency. Maturity. Abandonment of tradition. Change. | According to both sides, education intends to be critical of tradition: To question and to decide. | Preservation of tradition. Stagnation. |
| Development of the individual. Self-actualizing. | According to both sides, education helps the individual find its way and place in the society. | To fit into society and comm Self-sacrifice for economica social purpose. Hierarchy. S |

In conclusion to these statements, I understand education as primarily an attitude and not a specific action. It takes the risk of dialogical encounter between unequal but also equal partners (see table 5). According to Wanzenried (1996), it's a common and mutual movement of asking, searching, recognizing, forming, answering, changing, etc. It means a learning process on both sides. Teaching requires high presence and care. It asks for the willingness to reflect and to decide. It needs professional intervention and one's intuition for the fruitful moment. The educational effect is not feasible, but it occurs as a coincidental gift as a result of the encounter of two individuals. Teachers have to know about their own power and the permanent danger of misusing it. They have to be well acquainted with their individual constructive and destructive energies. They have to be conscious of boundaries, limits, and detachment regarding themselves, their role, their students, etc. They have to take changes between chaos and order with composure. They have to meet processes which are not under control of a human being with humility and confidence.

To end this chapter I want to introduce an analogy of Wanzenried (1996). He uses poetic language to describe education as an analogue to the art of dancing. Within the introduction to that poem he writes: "When I describe education as an art which risks balancing within the dialogical encounter, it's quite logical looking out for an analogy within the art of dancing. It remains the question to which form of dance: to the classical ballroom dance with its established forms and conventions; to the dance of the shamans with its ritual meaning; to the disco dance where individuals are dancing in common step; to the fiery Flamenco with its power and passion; to the classical ballet with its perfect figures and forms; to the dance improvisation with its surprises; or to the street dance with its artistic highlights? To every form of dancing I see its peculiar analogy."

**Education as an Analogue to the Art of Dancing**

Education is based on social conventions and interprets them
In its own way of guiding and following
As in ballroom dancing.

Education has its ritual meaning
As an introduction to a special culture
As the Shamanistic dance.

Education happens in interaction
Between individuals in community
As disco dancing.

Education needs vivid presence
And skilled movements
As ballet.

Education is grounded in deep emotions
As Flamenco.

Education needs to trust in intuition and the special moment
As dance improvisation.

Education means to go to the limits of what is possible
As street dance.

And finally, all of these forms, like education,
Create space and time,
Alternating movement and quiet, sound and silence.

Peter Wanzenried
(Translation by Decurtins, Hösli, Sherman, and Wanzenried)

## Chapter 5

# Concluding Reflections

I learned the intermodal method in a very heterogeneous context. My peers have been students of different age groups and different professions, with many different educational and personal backgrounds, intentions, and goals. But all of them have had an interest in pedagogy: People working in health service, at school and kindergarten, in social, therapeutical, or theological settings, etc. Together we've been introduced into the method in the described way, by experiencing prior activities on our age level, by reflections, and by theoretical inputs. Settings of supervision helped us to find ways to transfer the new learning into our personal working fields.

My field of research was limited to my specific working context. On the other hand, teachers who attended my inservice training courses transferred and applied the method very successfully into their specific educational contexts, and gained interesting experiences: They taught older or younger students; they taught classes, small groups, or individual students; they applied the method in classes with mainly German-speaking students and only a few non-German-speaking students, in speech therapy, in music education, in the education of deaf students.

My research and my reflection on the intermodal method heightens my conviction that it is an important and valuable contribution to education, specifically to teaching immigrant children. Further, I'm certain that the intermodal method can be very useful in many other borderline situations as well as in everyday school life. And what about applying this method with gifted children within either the regular context or in separate contexts? Which role the intermodal method will play in our lifetime which is characterized by overstimulation, where children are more or less learning by being in contact with a virtual secondhand world of television, computers, Internet, etc., instead of being in touch with the real world? Intermodal learning will be an important and useful contribution to education by offering a human and holistic counterpoint to the acquirement of knowledge through virtual mediums by supporting fantasy, gaining genuine understanding, by taking care of the primary needs of the students, and by taking care of the soul. Again, I care for the principle of the balance: "Nothing is poisonous. Everything is poisonous. It all depends on the dose" (see chapter 4). In other words: The introduction into and the application of the virtual mediums are important *as well as* the intermodal method, depending on the situation, the context, the needs, the intention, and the goal.

Within this book I described my way of learning, teaching, and thinking. I hope to inspire others searching for a personal way to translate into their individual working context what they have learned from the book. I hope that no immigrant child—no child at all—has to lose the ability to express him- or herself. I believe very strongly in every child.

I hope that you find to be this book an appropriate and useful contribution to multicultural education and to other aspects of education as well. I end this book by giving three impressive examples which emphasize the effectiveness and importance of the method of intermodal learning with immigrant children:

**Rafael**. We already know him (see p. 15). I always had the impression that he would be quite a bright boy. His weak side was poor concentration when doing mathematics or when writing. His reading ability was quite weak, but in mathematics he was above average. Even though he didn't proceed when he had the task to fulfill a certain group of calculations within one lesson, I had the impression that he was deep in thought. On the other hand, when he had problems to solve within an intermodal process, he showed an extended concentration and an ability of complex thinking. I was very happy that I learned about this side of Rafael. Here, a good relationship between us started to grow that could help us overcome difficult situations.

**Three girls from Senegal.** A teacher from an inservice training course told us one evening: "The girls, second and third grade, have been living in Zurich for five years, but they are still outsiders at our school. They refuse to write and to read, therefore they attend remedial teaching two times a week with me. I noticed their interests in glove puppets. That's why I let them choose a puppet and walk with it through the room. I gave the direction to get in contact with the puppet and to find out what it would like to tell. I said to the children that they had to write down the words immediately to make sure that the message wouldn't get lost. Soon after the beginning, the weakest girl came rushing to my desk and asked for her book. Then, she began to write a long text. Normally she didn't write anything. Now I know that she is able to write. I'm very happy about this."

**Nuran,** eleven years old, from Kurdistan. She hasn't seen her parents, her sister, and her brother for seven years. When her parents brought her to our class they

**Photograph 9:** Nuran as Cimona on Stage

declared that she was mentally retarded. She looked to me as an eight years old girl, tremendously shy and cautious. She used to live with her grandparents. She had never attended school. For a long time, she gave me the impression of refusing to learn German. The parents told me that she wouldn't eat, that she would cry a lot, that she would be mad. I had the idea that she was suffering greatly. At school I realized that she was quite attentive in observing what was going on. I realized that she was interested in numbers and letters, but she didn't talk. I also realized that she became inspired by other children rather than by adults. By being models, the children of the class helped her to express herself with colors, movements, and instruments. When making masks of plaster, she helped in a very mature manner. By gestures she declared her readiness to make her own mask. Finally, she created a very personal mask and performed on stage as Cimona with increasing self-confidence. She learned to read, to write, and to calculate up to one hundred within nine months. She learned to use colors, pencils, scissors, glue, etc. And finally she started speaking in German. I think that she started to find her place in the new environment.

# Appendix

The appendix shows the steps of the processes which appear in the book. The sequences could be transferred into any educational setting. Classes, groups, situations, and settings are all different, and therefore, the processes will develop in different ways in each setting. Further, you may find that a certain sequence is not suitable for your specific situation. This description of the courses is provided to further assist you in understanding my work. My objective is to motivate educators to search for opportunities to transfer these intermodal processes to one's own educational setting. The described processes are only a few out of many possible activities.

## 1. The Mask Project

The full class: The students attended the class for one to twelve months. During the process, one child left the class, and two children entered the class. The process took seventeen lesson periods (two hours each) from January through June.

### First Step: To Form the Masks (Eleven lesson periods)

1. I introduce the theme through a mask book; through pictures of my own masks; through pictures which show myself having a mask of plaster cast.
2. We make masks of plaster cast. For this we have two working places. (See also p. 30 and p. 38)
3. Onto the plaster masks we form masks of papier-mâché. This paper mask will become the final mask. First, we paint the masks of plaster cast with liquid soap, so that the two masks won't stick together. Second, we put one layer of papier-mâché onto the plaster mask, followed by a layer of thin gauze, add a second

layer of papier-mâché, a second layer of gauze, and a last layer of papier-mâché.

4. After three days, I separate the paper masks from the plaster masks. We finish the edges of the masks.
5. I show a book and some postcards with totem poles and masks of native Americans. With chalk we sketch masks.
6. We paint the inside and the outside of the masks with white acrylic paint.
7. We color the masks.
8. We glue hairs and other attributes. I cut slits in each mask to see through. We attach elastic bands. For some students, the mirror became an important partner.
9. The students have to find names for their masks. I give the following instructions: "Take your mask. Walk with the mask in your hand. Talk to your mask and listen to how your mask is talking. Talk with your mask in a fairy language. Ask your mask about its name. Write down the name or names."
10. The students have to find fitting clothes. My instructions: "Find some clothes which fit to your mask. The mask will help you find the right clothes. Dress up. The mirror will help you."

## Second Step: To Act on Stage (Six lesson periods)

*Overall Rules*

- The children should name their masks—if possible create a name rather than using an existing name (see above). Suitable alternatives: e.g., "sister or friend of Pocahontas"; "brother or friend of Batman"; etc.
- The first scene on stage should be an awakening ritual (see below).
- The masks should be worn only on stage. When not in use, the masks are lying on a cloth in front of the stage.
- Instruction to the students: When it's your turn to act on stage, take your mask, go onto the stage behind the curtain and put the mask on.
- Each scene begins and ends by a stroke of a Tibetan bell.
- After the final act on stage, before taking the masks home, a final ritual should be performed (see below).
- If there is no stage, the space for acting should be marked clearly on the floor (by tape or by a string).

*First Entrance: The Awakening Ritual*
Closed curtain. The child behind the curtain puts on his or her mask. The audience calls out the name of the mask three times. The mask enters through the curtain, introduces her- or himself by bowing three times. The child takes the mask off and leaves the stage.

*Second Entrance*
How does the mask walk?

1. Warm up by moving to piano music.
2. Experience of finding different ways to walk.
3. Ask your mask what its individual style of walking is.

Instruction: The mask should cross the stage and walk back to the starting point.

*Third Entrance*
Cross the stage different times by experiencing different kinds of steps. Which one is typical for your mask? (I give feedback by copying the way of walking which struck me most. My intention is to emphasize a special or new way of walking. This medium I use several times throughout the process to encourage the children to clarify their movements.)

*Fourth Entrance*
Repetition of the third entrance. (I motivate the masks to play, to use the offered space on stage.)

*Fifth Entrance*
I place seven different objects in front of the stage: Flowers, a piano chair, a string, a kalimba (an African instrument), a tambourine with bells, a newspaper, and an empty case. The instruction: Select the most fitting object for your mask, place it on the stage, and let your mask play with it.

*Sixth Entrance*
Repetition of the fifth entrance.

*Seventh Entrance*
Decide to go on stage with or without an object. What does your mask like best? Seven students decided to act without an object, five decided to

act with an object. (This time, every mask presents a very personal and explicit performance.)

*Preparation for the Final Performance*

- The beginning: Practicing of the introduction of the masks: All masks are called by their names in front of the curtain; bowing three times.
- The scenes: Clarifying the beginning of each performance.
- The end: Practicing the final bowing.

*Eighth Entrance: The Performance with an Audience*

Audience: Parents, sisters, brothers, and two other classes from our school.

*Finale*

1. Picture time on stage: Go on stage and pose in your best position. I take pictures of each mask.
2. Final ritual: We sit on the floor in a circle. A colored cloth is spread out in the middle. Every child says goodbye to her or his mask and puts it under the clothe.
3. The children take their masks home.

## 2. The Subject of Opposites

Four children, the advanced ones, have been in Switzerland for about ten months, two children have been in Switzerland for about two months. They speak French, which means that they can communicate with me. One child who neither understands nor speaks German has recently entered the class. The age of the children: 7–11 years. Native countries: Dominican Republic, Kosovo, Morocco, Sri Lanka, Turkey, Zaire. Duration: about 14, 16 language lessons.

1. Introducing and exercising about 20 pairs of opposites with the advanced students.
2. Repeating the words using a memory game (for each picture and word) together with the beginners.
3. Walking about in the room, acting out the opposites: slow–fast; large–small; round–angular; sad–happy; bright–dark; day–night; bad–nice; heavy–lightweight, etc.
   1st phase: All children represent the same things.

2nd phase: Two groups, each group representing the opposite (→ simultaneous experience of opposed elements). During the two phases, the groups switch opposites whenever I ring a bell.

4. Each child selects a pair of opposites. I gave pictures of day and night (sun and moon with stars) to the new child. Task: Find musical instruments with which these opposites can be expressed. (One or two instruments may be sufficient to express the opposites.) This phase requires much time and support on the part of the teacher. The teacher may have to present an example, live or from a tape recorder.
5. Play the opposites; make a tape recording at the same time.
6. Listen to the recordings. Evaluation by the child and by the group: Did the music meet the intention? If necessary, new recordings should be made until a satisfactory result is obtained.
7. Optional but difficult step: Two children try duets with a pair of opposites (→ simultaneous expression of opposed elements).
8. Painting the chosen opposites. Introduction: Listen to the music and move with it. Shape of the sheets: Large circular areas (approximately 3 feet in diameter), subdivided and cut into quarters or sixths, depending on the number of children. Each child paints two opposite segments of the circle.
9. Examining the painted work: Two children absent during the painting try to associate the words used with the pictures (important step: finding symbols for best possible general recognition). Discussion and possibly adjustment or even creation of new pictures.
10. To deepen the process: Create round areas (approximately 12 inches in diameter) to be painted on both sides with a pair of opposites (the *two sides of a coin*). Verify the results by identifying the pairs of opposites in the group. This phase can also include a guessing game.
11. Possibly make adjustments. Inscribe the round areas and hang them from the ceiling in such a way that they can turn.

During the whole process, the advanced group also did writing and grammatical work on the subject of opposites.

### Selecting the Subject

The subject of *opposites* is an example of a learning subject that can have an important educational effect since it involves a principle of life:

ambivalence, as well as dualism. This is an issue that is present everywhere and which has always interested philosophers, psychologists, and mankind in general.

The method of intermodal learning is not merely about developing a vocabulary, but each child will have new experiences which go far beyond the acquisition of a second language. It means working on the foundation on which language in general—mother tongue and foreign language—can develop. The new children were able to follow quite well and learned many new words.

## 3. Intermodal Processes

### Working with Clay

The full class: The children have been in the class for two to eight months. New children joined during the process. The process duration was four lesson periods (two hours each).

I think that it is important to work with clay. The soft, humid, and elastic material relaxes and brings subtle things to light. Intensive familiarization with the material is essential. This happens in play. Many things are created accidentally: foodstuff, houses, animals, babies, children, volcanoes, balls, pots, etc. The things created are shown around and named spontaneously. Playing with clay evokes inner stories, building bridges to the individual worlds.

Location: The cellar; the caretaker covered the floor with a plastic sheet; we worked standing at tables. Each child receives a good size piece of clay (22 pounds for 12 persons).

1. First afternoon: I ask the children to play with the material, which is new to most of them. I myself work with it, too, kneading, beating, rolling, forming the clay. However, I do not create any figured shapes. My shapes change continuously. I want to be a model for the children who initially act in a restrained way in most cases. My own playing animates the children to play.
2. I have the children work with the clay with their eyes closed for about five minutes. Some of the children stay with it much longer. At the end of the lesson, all the clay is formed into lumps and stored away together.
3. Second afternoon: At first everybody tries to form a ball with their eyes closed. Free transition to play. Then they have time to play individually or with someone else.

4. Third afternoon: The play is resumed; the new children are introduced to the material. We then begin the creation of a product which is to be dried, baked, and painted.
5. Introduction into the basic rules of the work with clay: Work from one piece; spread well. Now the children need intensive help. Some of the objects must be cut apart, made hollow, and put together again.
6. Allow the objects to dry and have them baked.
7. Fourth afternoon: Painting the objects with acrylic paint.

**Process: Picture → Text → Music → Picture**

Six children who have been in Switzerland for nearly a year. During the first lesson, another two female students join. The process takes place during 10 German lessons: This is Monday morning following the holidays. After the welcome and a brief conversation:

1. Remember your holidays. Remember the Friday before your holidays. (We had worked with clay for the second time then.) What would you like to paint right now? The children paint their pictures. (Meanwhile, the two new students enter.)
2. Hanging the pictures on the blackboard. Looking at the pictures. The children tell what they painted. They ask questions. Dialogues about the pictures take place. Rafael's volcano meets with vivid interest.
3. Write down some sentences about your picture on a sheet of paper. ( I rewrite the sentences in correct German.)
4. Looking at lava stone and a book about volcanoes.
5. Looking at the pictures. Each child reads his/her sentence.
6. Task: Write the sentences down on a colored sheet in the form you want it. Attach the sheet to your picture with glue. (In the meantime, the two new students paint a picture. I write appropriate words and sentences for them to copy about their pictures. One of the girls writes about her picture in both her native language and in German.)
7. Task: Take your sentences home and learn to read them.
8. From now on, the new children also take part in the common process. Each child presents his/her picture with the text to the class. I read the texts of the new children aloud and they repeat.
9. Musical instruments are ready at hand. Task: What is the most beautiful thing or the thing you like the most about your picture?

How does it sound? Try to find the best sound. I demonstrate this task using another person's picture as an example.

10. Presentation of the sounds, with the picture forming the score.
11. We get the musical instruments of the previous day again. I play on each instrument and demonstrate possibilities of differentiated playing. All texts are read again. Then we practice with the instruments.
12. Repetition of the music played with the pictures. Recording the music on a tape. Listening to the tape recordings.
13. Each child receives two large sheets which she/he divides into three parts of the same size (one part for each piece of music. Task: Paint the pieces of music with a piece of chalk: Listen to a piece of music—a break to complete the picture—listen to the second piece of music—a break to complete the picture—etc. (I myself paint as well so that the children can overcome their insecurity.)
14. Looking at the results. I review the entire process with the children. The children decide to bind the pictures in a book to take home.

## Example of Contact with Professional Art

The full class. The children have been in the class for different periods. Objective: establish a contact to the art of adults, to the "world of professionals" using *Peter and the Wolf* by Serge Prokofiew as an example. Duration: 3 lessons. Half of the children have already set to music some of their own pictures.

The contact with professional art provides the children for their work a foundation to and promotes self-esteem: "What I am doing makes sense. Adults set pictures and stories to music themselves." Their own previous activity (e.g., creating music for a picture, transforming persons and figures into movement) deepens the process and furthers the understanding of music. The result is great joy and satisfaction.

1. Telling the story of *Peter and the Wolf* from the picture book.
2. In the singing room: Name the persons and figures of the book. Associate pictures and names.
3. Transform persons and figures into movements and sounds. If necessary I extend this, for example, by asking: How does a cat creep up to a bird?
4. The children lie down on the floor. I play the original music for each person and each figure twice (without words).

5. When listening for the third time, we try to associate the music with the persons and figures.
6. Back in the classroom: Listening to the full story and showing the picture book at the same time. Whoever wants, has the opportunity to make a drawing about it.
7. The children turns taking the book and the music cassette home to listen to again.

# Notes

1 The statement was passed on to me by word of mouth. It goes back to Paolo Freire.

2 Here, the German word is *musse*, the meaning of which is very similar to the qualities of mediation. *Musse* means time to be, to be at peace; an opportunity and a possibility to do anything. The first quality of such a doing is a nondirective state. "At the sight of nothing, the soul rejoices" (Moore, 1994b, p. 4).

3 All names are changed to respect the children's integrity.

4 Albanian: Kosova; actually a part of Yugoslavia, which is longing for autonomy.

5 Now called Democratic Republic of Congo.

6 For this and all following interviews, I chose the method of self-interviewing to clarify my work. K stays for my middle name, Katharina. It is a second voice of myself who asks questions of E, Elisabeth.

# Bibliography

Berger-Kündig, P. (1996). *Unpublished papers to the object "Working with Core Ideas."* Köln, Germany: Author.

Bollnow, O. F. (1959). *Existenzphilosophie und Pädagogik* [Existentialism and education]. Stuttgart, Berlin, Köln, Mainz; Germany: W. Kohlhammer Verlag.

———. (1987). *Vom Geist des Übens. Eine Rückbesinnung auf elementare didaktische Erfahrungen* [About the spirit of exercise. A reflection on elementary didactic experiences]. Oberwil b. Zug, Switzerland: Verlag Rolf Kugler. (Revised and reprint; first published in 1978).

Buber, M. (1983). *Ich und Du* [Me and you] (11th ed.). Heidelberg, Germany: Schneider

———. (1995). *Reden über Erziehung* [Lectures about education] (8th ed.). Heidelberg, Germany: Schneider. (Reprint; first published in 1953).

Cummins, J. (1980). The entry and exit fallacy in bilingual education. *NABE Journal*, 4 (pp. 25–60).

———. (1984). *Bilingualism and Special Education: Issues in Assessment and Pedagogy.* Clevedon, Avon, England: Multilingual Matters Ltd.

Donaldson, M. (1978). *Children's Minds.* Glasgow: Collins.

Egger, B. (1984). *Entwicklung der bildnerischen Sprache und des bildnerischen Ausdrucks* [Development of the figurative language and the figurative expression]. Bern, Switzerland: Zytglogge.

Erikson, E. H. (1994). *The Life Cycle Completed* (reissued). New York, London: W. W. Norton & Company.

Erziehungsdirektion des Kantons Zürich. (1991). *Lehrplan für die Volksschule des Kantons Zürich* [Curriculum for elementary and high school of the Canton of Zurich]. Zürich, Switzerland: Lehrmittelverlag des Kantons Zürich.

Erziehungsrat des Kantons Zürich. (1995). *Empfehlungen zur Schulung der fremdsprachigen Kinder und zur interkulturellen Pädagogik* [Recommendation for the education of non-German speaking children and for inter-cultural education]. Zürich, Switzerland: Author.

Gardner, H. (1991). *The Unschooled Mind: How Children Think and How Schools Should Teach.* New York: Basic Books.

———. (1993a). *Frames of Mind: The Theory of Multiple Intelligences* (2nd ed.). New York: Basic Books.

———. (1993b). *Creative Minds. An Anatomy of Creativity Seen Through the Lives of Freud, Einstein, Picasso, Stravinsky, Eliot, Graham and Gandhi.* New York: Basic Books.

Ginn, V. (1991). *Geister der Erde* [The spirited earth] (A. Michalowski, Trans.). Munich, Germany: Metamorphosis Verlag. (Original work published 1990).

Grünewald, D., & Benkel, A. (1996). Maske und Maskenspiel [Mask and mask performing]. *Kunst und Unterricht, Zeitschrift für Kunstpädagogik* [Art and education, journal for art education]. Seelze, Germany: Erhard Friedrich Verlag.

Gudjons, H. (1995). *Pädagogisches Grundwissen* [Educational basic knowledge] (4th ed.). Bad Heilbrunn, Germany: Verlag Julius Klinkhardt.

von Hentig, H. (1996). *Bildung* [Education]. München, Germany & Wien, Austria: Hanser Verlag.

Herzka, H. St. (1989). *Die neue Kindheit: Dialogische Entwicklung—autoritätskritische Erziehung* [The new childhood: Dialogue development—critical of authority in education]. Basel, Switzerland: Schwabe.

Hösli, E., & Wanzenried, P. (1997). Pädagogik als Kunst: eine Chance für das Unterrichten in Krisensituationen? [Education as an art: An opportunity for education in borderline situations?] *Schweizer Schule, 10/97* [Swiss school, 10/97] (pp. 3–9).

Huser, J. (1999). Was heisst da "hochbegabt"? [What's the meaning of being "highly gifted"?] *triangel, 1/1999* (pp. 5–6). Zürich, Switzerland: Schul- und Sportdepartement.

Kegan, R. (1996). *The Evolving Self: Problem and Process in Human Development* (13th ed.). Cambridge, Massachusetts, and London, England: Harvard University Press.

Knill, P. (1979). *Ausdruckstherapie: Künstlerischer Ausdruck in Therapie und Erziehung als intermediale Methode* [Expressive therapy: Intermodal learning therapy and education]. Lilienthal, Germany: Eres.

———. (1983). *Medien in Therapie und Ausbildung* [Media in therapy and teaching]. Suderburg, Germany: Ohlsen.

Knill, P., Nienhaus, & B., Fuchs, M. (1995). *Minstrels of Soul: Intermodal Expressive Therapy*. Toronto, Ontario: Palmerston Press.

Lanfranchi, A. (1996). Unterwegs zur multikulturellen Gesellschaft [On the way to a multicultural society]. *Zeitschrift für Migration und soziale Arbeit 3/4* (pp. 30–37).

Lanfranchi, A., & Hagmann, Th. (Eds.). (1992). *Immigrantenkinder, Plädoyer für eine integrative Pädagogik* [Immigrant children, a plea for integrative education]. Lucerne, Switzerland: Edition SZH, HPS-Reihe 5.

Lommel, L. (1970). *Masken—Gesichter der Menschheit* [Masks—faces of humanity]. Zurich, Switzerland: Atlantis Verlag.

Moore, T. (1994a). *Care of the Soul*. New York: Harper Perennial. (Original work published in 1992).

———. (1994b). *Meditations on the Monk Who Dwells in Daily Life*. New York: Harper Collins.

Nodari, C. (1989). *Deutsch für fremdsprachige Kinder; Theoretischer Teil; Grundlagen für den Unterricht* [German for children with a foreign mother tongue; theoretical part; basis for teaching]. Aarau, Switzerland: Interkantonale Lehrmittelzentrale, Lehrmittelverlag des Kantons Aargau.

Nold, W. (ca. 1993). *Das Spiel der Masken* [The play of the masks]. Moers, Germany: Edition Aragon.

Ohlsen, I. (1994). *Einschulung fremdsprachiger Kinder und Jugendlicher im Kanton Zürich* [Starting school of non-German speaking children and young people in the Canton of Zurich]. Winterthur & Zürich, Switzerland: Schulamt der Stadt Winterthur & Pädagogische Abteilung der Erziehungsdirektion, Sektor Ausländerpädagogik.

Piaget, J. (1970). *Psychologie der Intelligenz* [Psychology of the intelligence]. Zürich, Switzerland: Rascher Paperback.

Riemer, C. (1986). *Maskenbau und Maskenspiel* [Mask building and mask performing]. Kiel, Germany: Moby Dick.

———. (1992) *Masken und andere Gesichte* [Masks and other visions]. Kiel, Germany: Moby Dick.

Ruf, U., & Gallin, P. (1996). Sich einlassen und eine Sprache finden—Merkmale einer interaktiven und fächerübergreifenden Didaktik [To get involved and find language—Characteristics of an interactive and inter-subjective teaching method]. In Voss, R. (Ed.), *Die Schule neu erfinden* (pp. 154–177). Germany: Luchterhand.

Shuy, R. W. (1978). Problems in assessing language ability in bilingual education programs. In Lafontaine, H., Persky, H., & Golubchick, L. (Eds.): *Bilingual Education*. Wayne, New Jersey: Avery Publishing Group, Inc.

———. (1981). Conditions affecting language learning and maintenance among Hispanics in the United States. *NABE Journal*, 6 (pp. 1–18).

Türk, M. (Ed.) (1997). *Ich besiege alle Drachen! Künstlerische und therapeutische Arbeit mit Flüchtlingskindern* [I conquer all dragons! Artistic and therapeutic work with refugee children]. Bad Honeff, Germany: Horlemann Verlag.

Urbanski, R. (1994). *Maskenbau—Schminken—Eigene Maske* [Mask building—make-up—one's own mask]. Moers, Germany: Edition Aragon.

Wanzenried, P. (1996). *Unpublished papers for ISIS program "Art for Learning."* Winterthur, Switzerland: Author.

Wygotski, L. S. (1974). *Denken und Sprechen* [Vygotsky, L.: Thought and Language]. Frankfurt, Germany: Fischer Verlag.

Printed by
CPI books GmbH, Leck

Zeitfracht Medien GmbH
Ferdinand-Jühlke-Straße 7
99095 Erfurt, Deutschland
produktsicherheit@kolibri360.de